1

Published by Moon Leaf Publishing

Publication date 2021

ISBN: 978-0-9997612-5-0 (sc)

ISBN: 978-0-9997612-6-7 (hc)

www.sdmooreauthor.com

INTRODUCTION

When I initially became interested in writing screenplays I found that screenwriting books were written for someone who already had advanced knowledge of the craft. The books used many esoteric terms that are foreign to the world of book writing. Authors of screenwriting books simply weren't reaching me as a writer who tells stories through books.

I also thought about going to film school, but after nearly completing a doctorate, there was no way that I was going to attend four more years of college courses, nor was I going to amass a huge load of new college debt. It was only through years of trial, error and triumph that I figured things out.

My goal is to give my fellow authors the simple tools needed to write a movie script. This book also has bonus features like quizzes, writer's block removal exercises, pitch deck training and my cash award winning autobiographic feature script - Stronger When She's Broken.

Screenwriting for Storytellers is a must have tool for anyone who wants to turn their story into a movie script. Now let's get started.

PART ONE
THE
BASICS

MARGINS AND PAGE NUMBERS

Screenwriting software and templates in word processing applications will have the margins set for script format. Otherwise:

- Top, bottom and right margins at 1"
- Left margin at 1.25
- CHARACTER <u>centered</u> with left indent at 1.25" and right indent at 1"
- Dialogue <u>left aligned</u> with left indent at 1.75" and right indent at 1.5"
- **<u>Please check margin requirements before submitting to an entity.</u>**

Name of Screenplay

By

S.L. Moe

PAGE NUMBERS

1. No page number goes on the cover page.

2. The first page of the script begins with the <u>transition</u> words **FADE IN:** in the right corner.

3. Page numbers begin on sheet of paper number three, with the number 2 in the upper right hand corner.
4. All page numbers thereafter will be placed in the upper right hand corner.

SCRIPT ELEMENTS

There are many software programs that will automatically format a script, but you need to know the basic elements of a script and where those elements should be located.

```
EXT. BOOKSTORE - NOON                                        SCENE HEADING

Remnants of an early snowfall melts on the streets.

Julz and Jaxx meet up with their mother CONNIE (late fifties,
race-Black).                                                 ACTION

Connie is standing in a line on the sidewalk in front of a
bookstore.

                    JULZ AND JAXX                            CHARACTER
                     (in unison)                             (PARENTHETICAL)
             Hi Mom!                                         DIALOGUE
```

```
EXT. BOOKSTORE - NOON

Remnants of an early snowfall melts on the streets.

Julz and Jaxx meet up with their mother CONNIE (late fifties,
race-Black).

Connie is standing in a line on the sidewalk in front of a
bookstore.

                    JULZ AND JAXX
                     (in unison)
             Hi Mom!
```

NOTES: _____

_____

_____

SCENE HEADINGS AKA SLUGLINES

A scene heading is inserted at the beginning of a new scene. The beginning of a scene heading denotes interior (INT.), exterior (EXT.) or simultaneous interior and exterior location (INT/ENT.). The middle states the specific location. The end gives the time of day.

See the following examples:

EXT. DAVID'S HOME - NIGHT

EXT. HOT SPRINGS – DAY

INT. SPACE FIGHTER – NIGHT (YEAR 3025)

EXT. MONSTER'S LAIR – DAY

Use Interior/Exterior to identify when the camera can simultaneously shoot a scene in the interior/exterior of a location (cab of truck, jet, etc.).

INT/EXT. SCOTT'S CAR – DAY

INT/EXT. MOUNTAIN TRAM - DAY

INT/EXT. HELICOPTER COCKPIT – DUSK

INT/EXT. FREIGHT ELEVATOR - NIGHT

NOTES:

_____

_____

_____

MINI SCENE HEADINGS

What if you have multiple scenes in one location such as a home, museum or hospital? In the past a screenwriter would use scene transitions like "CUT TO," but the contemporary method is to use a Mini Scene Heading to transition between locations in the same dwelling. For example:

INT. JULZ'S APARTMENT - DAY

HOME OFFICE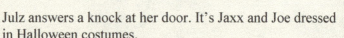

Julz puts on virtual reality gloves and slips on her V/R goggles to bring up the image of Mr. Smith's misspelled tattoo in virtual reality. She uses her fingers, hands, and eyebrows to manipulate the commands on the screen.

Julz sketches out ideas in virtual reality.

She repeatedly tries new designs, but nothing feels right. She sighs with frustration before shutting things down for the day.

LIVINGROOM - NIGHT

Julz answers a knock at her door. It's Jaxx and Joe dressed in Halloween costumes.

NOTES:

_____

_____

_____

ACTION

The action element of the script describes what's happening in the scene. Often descriptions in the ACTION element are written short and to the point. The bottom line, keep it brief. ACTION should be written in **present tense.** The writer should also avoid giving directing and/or music cues.

Below are some simple action lines.

The ladies stop dancing.

A sixty-year-old attractive White man wearing a flat top gambler's hat gets out of large red pickup truck. A sign painted on the side of the truck reads, Sumner's Industrial Construction.

SUMNER Havreaux enters the ink shop. He's carrying two medium sized boxes.

Sumner speaks with a relaxed Cajun drawl.

ACTION: VISUAL

Authors use narration to help readers imagine various objects and settings in a story. Screenwriters use the action element to indicate what visual items should appear on the screen

For instance, an author would use narration to tell readers that a man is standing on a riverbank in front of Mount Rainier and then go on to describe the color of the sky, whether the sky is clear or cloudy, the brightness of the sun, beauty of the landscape and colors of the rainbow.

A screenwriter uses the scene heading to show the location and an action element to define the setting.

EXT. HOT SPRINGS - NIGHT

After a short drive Julz and David can see glimmers of colored lights between the peaks of the mountains.

Julz and David get out of the vehicle near a trail leading to one of the dipping areas of the lake sized body of water. They stand in awe of the sight of the bright green and red bands of the Aurora Borealis dancing in the sky.

Colorful bands of the Aurora Borealis are so bright that they paint the mountains with beautiful waves of red and green light.

The waves of light reveal a frozen water fall and big horned sheep stair stepped along the cliffs in the darkness.

ACTION: AUDIBLE

Another component of a film is sound or silence. Again a book writer uses narration to help readers imagine what things sound like in a story. Screenwriters use the action element to convey sound cues in a screenplay.

Here are some examples:

- Jack hears car tires screech just before a car crashes into a street lamp.

- A glass shattering on the marble floor breaks the silence.

- Muffled techno music can be heard outside of the club.

- The dog jumps at the sudden sound of loud, roaring thunder.

- Children laugh and playfully squeal on the playground.

- The drummer bangs her drumsticks together four times before the band begins to play.

- The sound of hooves from a single horse drawn carriage echoes in the night.

- Joe uses a stick to stir the crackling campfire.

- Large chunks of hail crash against the roof of Kate's car.

- Douglas stands on the pier listening to the sound of waves crashing against the shore.

LESSON ANALYSIS #1

Let's analyze the previous section. You've learned about the basic elements of screenplay structure, scene headings and writing action. How do you think those elements of a screenplay will challenge you as a writer?

NOTES:

_____

_____

_____

_____

_____

_____

_____

_____

_____

_____

_____

_____

_____

CHARACTER

The character is the name of the entity doing the talking. A character can be a person, job title (Head Chef) or object (robot) doing the talking. However, the first time a character's name is introduced in a script that name must be CAPITALIZED. For example:

> **JULZ** washes down her meds with a cup of punch. She fluffs her long curly hair in a large mirror in the lobby.
>
> Shop assistants **DAISY** and **TERRA** arrive.
>
> > DAISY AND TERRA
> > Morning Julz!
>
> > JULZ
> > Morning ladies.
>
> The rest of the Havreaux sisters, **JAXX, JADE** and **JOE** enter the tattoo shop.

NOTES:

_____

_____

_____

DIALOGUE

Dialogue is the vehicle through which a character speaks. A character's name or title appears above the dialogue component. Dialogue is placed in a script without quotations. **For example:**

> JULZ
> Morning.
>
> DAVID GREENE
> This is my good friend and agent Youngblood.
>
> Youngblood stands up and nods to Julz.
>
> DAVID GREENE
> I hope that you like the stuff I picked out for you.
> JULZ
> Everything is very nice thank you.
>
> DAVID GREENE
> The guy in the kitchen is my brother Ronnie.
> KITCHEN
>
> RONNIE waves hello to Julz.
>
> RONNIE
> I picked out the orange blossom soaps and feminine wash.
> LIVINGROOM
> JULZ
> Thank you that was very thoughtful. Now I'm orange blossom fresh from my rooter to my tooter.

DIALOGUE CONTINUED: (O.S.)

Off Screen (O.S.) is used when a character is speaking out of view of the camera. Below are two examples of how (O.S.) can be used:

Julz turns around and sees a set of black and pink lady's active wear laying on a bench at the foot of the bed. A note is sitting on top of the clothing.

She silently reads the note.

                    DAVID GREENE (O.S.)
                    Julz, please feel free to use the shower. I sent
                    my friend out to pick up some fresh clothes and
                    lady toiletries. Come on out and have breakfast
                    when you're ready. David

                    DAVID GREENE
                    Your costume is in the dryer and Ronnie removed
          your clothes.
                    JULZ
                    Great! Now more people have seen my T and A.

                    RONNIE
                    (yells from kitchen)
                    Don't worry girl. Your T and A are safe with
                    me. I'm strictly into tall guys with money. Know
                    your value girl. Get with the ones who will upgrade
                    your worth.

David walks over to a console and presses a button. A partition slides to cut off the kitchen from the living room and dining area.

                    RONNIE (O.S.)
                    Man don't be like that! You know how nosey
                    we are.

DIALOGUE CONTINUED: (V.O.)

Voice Over (V.O) is commonly used during phone conversations or when a character does the narration. Here's a sample of a phone message:

> DAVID GREENE
> Don't worry they know where you're at.
> Listen to the message your family left on my
> phone. David plays a message for Julz that was
> left on his phone by her mother and sisters.
>
> CONNIE (V.O.)
> (over phone's speaker)
> Julz this is your Mom. Please call me because
> we're worried about you. On second thought
> don't call because you are an adult and we trust
> you to do the right thing, but we're worried.
>
> JAXX (V.O.)
> (over phone's speaker)
> Listen horror writer, if anything happens to my
> sister, we'll cut off your little berries and press
> them in one of your books!
>
> CONNIE (V.O.)
> (over phone's speaker)
> And that's with a butter knife too.
>
> JADE AND JOE (V.O.)
> (over phone's speaker)
> We love you Julz!
>
> Julz slaps her forehead with the palm of her left hand.

DIALOGUE CONTINUED: (V.O.) PT2

Here's an example of Voice Over used as narration inside of a **Flashback**:

> DAVID GREENE
> I was a Captain in the Air Force when it
> happened.
>
> FLASHBACK:
>
> INT/EXT. MILITARY HELICOPTER - NIGHT
>
> David is in a military helicopter flying at night. He is sitting in a
> seat behind the pilot.
>
> DAVID GREENE (V.O.)
> I was on one of two helicopters on a night
> training mission in the desert.
>
> David adjusts his night vision goggles.
>
> DAVID GREENE (V.O.)
> We were on a training exercise to tighten up our
> skills to rescue people at night in rugged desert
> terrain.
>
> Karl Youngblood is sitting on the right side of the pilot in the
> same military helicopter as David.
>
> DAVID GREENE (V.O.)
> Sometimes I'm the co-pilot, but on that day my
> buddy Youngblood took the seat instead.
>
> A Military helicopter is flying adjacent to the one David is in.
> The pilot radios to David's copter, but his voice is frantic and
> garbled.
>
> DAVID GREENE (V.O.)
> Everything was going fine until something went
> wrong with the other copter.

PARENTHETICAL

The average author may not have heard of the term parenthetical. It's an element sometimes used in screenplays. A parenthetical is placed in (parentheses) under a character's name, but above a character's dialogue. A parenthetical is occasionally used to give direction to actors. It lets them know that they should express a particular attitude if there isn't a context within the dialogue or engage in a certain action while the character is speaking. Since parentheticals are used to give an actor direction, they should be used sparingly. Limiting parenthetical usage also aides in the smooth read of the script. For example:

> **SHARNIA VALDANA**
> (deep sultry voice)
> My name is Sharnia Valdana. I have
> a consultation appointment with
> Dr. Jaxxelle Havreaux.

*****

> **PREPPER DAN**
> (southern drawl)
> Hey cutie I'm thirsty. You want
> something to drank? I got beer,
> ale and lager.

*****

> **DAVID GREENE**
> (nervous)
> Happy Holidays Mrs. Havreaux. Hide
> all of the sharp knives because the
> scary horror writer is here. Haha!

> **RONNIE**
> (whispers to David)
> And the butter knives too.

PARENTHETICAL CONTINUED

Unless a film is purely driven by narration, action lines will show and within limits, the characters will tell the audience what's happening in each scene. Characters (actors) can relay the temperature they're experiencing, how things smell, how things feel, what things taste like, their frustrations, etc. However, a writer doesn't want to give too much direction in the way an actor should deliver a scene. One must allow actors to act. Here is a light hearted example that shows how dialogue helps to drive a character's attitudes without using a parenthetical:

                    CONNIE
          Isn't this a lovely day? Just when
          I thought the weather on this beautiful
          fall day couldn't get any better, Mother
          Nature bats her eye lashes and paints the
          mountains with a gorgeous rainbow.

          Look at the smiling faces walking
          around downtown. They can feel it too.
          It makes standing outside in this long
          line heavenly.
                    JAXX
          Geez Mom you're starting to sound like
          a hippie.
                    CONNIE
          Can't you girls feel the positive energy
          tingling through you?

                    JAXX
          What I feel tingling through me is the
          urge to tinkle.

BAD EXPOSITION

In screenwriting you'll hear the phrase "SHOW DON'T TELL."
There's no need to have characters explain the backstory through
dialogue when it can easily be shown on the screen. The writer
should expose backstory through patient story telling.

Exposition can happen when the story is too big for the structure of
the script so a screenwriter tries to cram as much backstory into the
script as possible. It's like trying to slipper horn a refrigerator into
the trunk of a car.

Exposition also happens when a writer wants to rush as much of the
backstory as possible into the first ten to fifteen pages because they
are trying to wow a producer. What results is an early, awkward
summary of the entire story told through the dialogue of the
characters.

Exposition can also happen when a character is used to give the
entire backstory of another character. This usually happens during a
conversation between characters. A screenwriter makes this error to
again cram in backstory through character dialogue.

However, a character occasionally giving too much backstory
information in a comedy can be a funny flaw, but exposition or
T.M.I. in a dramatic script, is just a flaw.

CHRIS
How's your sister doing?

KELLY
She's fine now, but she had her kidney removed
and now she can barely walk. She'll be moving
in with me in a month so she can work on her
Master's thesis – again. She's trying to get back
on that horse after putting off her degree to be
with her loser boyfriend, but now things are
looking up for her. She's no longer mad at me.

LESSON ANALYSIS #2

So far we've covered:

- Scene Headings and Slug Lines

- Action

- Character

- Parenthetical

- Dialogue Options

As a storyteller, you've likely noticed that script structure is designed with brevity in mind. Script structure forces a writer to deliver a heavy impact in under thirty-thousand words.

Let's analyze the previous sample scene featuring Connie and her daughter Jaxx. The audience can tell from Connie's attitude that she is having a great day and that she is fine with standing outside in a long line. The example shows that Action and Dialogue can be used instead of using a Parenthetical.

NOTES:

_____

_____

_____

TRANSITIONS

Let's dive deeper into other ways scenes transition. Transitions are used to switch between scenes, indicate changing settings, the passage of time and more. Below are the most commonly used screenplay transitions.

FADE IN: Is used at the very beginning of a screenplay.

> FADE IN:

CUT TO: Was used in older screenplays, but the contemporary method used to transition between most scenes and settings is to use SCENE HEADINGS OR SLUG LINES. For example:

INT. MOVIE THEATER - NIGHT

Jade is sitting a theater next to her boyfriend Scott watching a movie. She sees a text from Joelle telling her that Dan had a seizure, is unconscious and that she is trapped in his bedroom. Jade and Scott rush out of the movie theater.

Scott drives Jade to Prepper Dan's house.

INT/EXT. SCOTT'S CAR - NIGHT

Jade calls Joe.

> JADE
> (worried)
> We're on our way!

INT. PREPPER DAN'S BEDROOM - NIGHT

> JOE
> Oh thank goodness! With all of the parties and Mayhem tonight you guys will probably arrive before the ambulance gets here.

TRANSITIONS: FLASHBACKS

When using a Flashback make sure to use the appropriate scene heading and transition element.

BEGINNING A FLASHBACK:

> **BEGIN FLASHBACK:**
>
> INT/EXT. MILITARY HELICOPTER - NIGHT
>
> David is in a military helicopter flying at night. He is sitting in a seat behind the pilot.
>
> **OR**
>
> INT/EXT. MILITARY HELICOPTER - NIGHT **(FLASHBACK)**
>
> David is in a military helicopter flying at night. He is sitting in a seat behind the pilot.

ENDING A FLASHBACK:

> DAVID GREENE
> That's all I remember. He said that I saved his life, but he actually saved mine.
>
> **END FLASHBACK.**
>
> INT. EXAM ROOM AT TATTOO SHOP – MORNING
>
> DAVID GREENE
> As you can see, the doctors were able to save my leg.

TRANSITIONS: DISSOLVE TO

Dissolve to is used to convey the passage of long periods of time such as the next day, week, breakfast to dinner. For example:

INT. SHALANN'S BEDROOM - DAY

ShaLann sits in front of her laptop finishing up a brownie and a couple of shots of Remy on ice.

She stares at the computer screen.

> SHALANN (V.O.)
> Where should I begin? Oh, I know.

DISSOLVE

TO:

BEGIN PRIMARY FLASHBACK.

INT/EXT. TAXI CAB - DAY (1986)

It's a hot summer day.

Twenty-two-year-old ShaLann stares out of a partially opened rear window during her ride in the backseat of a taxi. She's cute, five-foot-three with a complexion about the tone of ten drops of cream in cup of black coffee.

Traffic is stalled at an intersection due to road construction.

NOTES:

_____

_____

_____

TRANSITIONS: THE MONTAGE

What if a screenwriter wants to use a series of short scenes in a flashback or wants to display a sequence of photos? The screenwriter may want to use a montage. For example:

INT. FLIGHTCREW WAR ROOM - DAY

A Colonel stands in front of a large wall map of the Middle East with a wood pointer. He briefs a large group of flight crew members about their pending mission.

EXT. AIR FORCE FLIGHTLINE - DAY

BEGIN MONTAGE.

Air Force flight crews race to their fighter jets.

Air Force crews load missiles onto fighter jets.

One by one fighter jets take to the skies.

END MONTAGE.

NOTES:

_____

_____

_____

PART TWO

QUIZ
TIME

QUIZ

Now let's see what you've learned. Don't peek at the answers.

1. What's wrong with this ***action*** statement? Tina tripped and broke her leg.
ANSWER:

_____

2. Write the following in script format: "Johnny is running late." Brad replied.

ANSWER:

_____

_____

3. What is the following script element called?
                    INT - RESTAURANT – DAY

ANSWER:

_____

_____

4. The character Julz states, "Oh man I'm exhausted." What script component should you use to indicate that she is yawning while talking? Circle the correct answer.
ANSWER: Transition   Parenthetical   Action   Scene Heading

5. Write the following dialogue in script format: Julz yawns as she says, "Oh man I'm exhausted."

ANSWER:

_____

_____

6. Select the scene element that describes the following: Calvin turns on the overhead light in the cab of his semi-truck.

ANSWER: Transition   Parenthetical   Action   Scene Heading

7. Use the correct scene heading to state the following location in script format: Sitting inside of the cab of a semi-truck at night.

ANSWER:

---

8. Adapt the following into script format:

"Awesome! I'm starving." Jade says.
 "Me too!" Daisy says as she grabs a plate.
Joe pours a jar of cheese sauce into a plastic serving bowl and then sticks a plastic spoon in the dip.
"*Joe!*" Julz shouts.

"What? Nobody wants to mess around with mom's fancy, smancy sauce pots anyway.

ANSWER:

PART THREE

The Art of

Story

to

Script

THE STORY TO SCRIPT PROCESS

I used to teach in the arenas of military, college, university and private business. During my years of teaching I learned three principles:

1) Keep it lean

2) Keep it simple

3) Keep it relevant

In this section we will apply those same principles to the process of converting your story into a movie script.

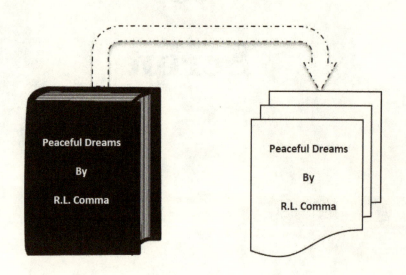

Principle #1 Keep It Lean

I'm sure that you wondered why some stories convert from book to script well, but some don't. What I learned is that the longer the original story is, the harder it is to adapt it into a screenplay. It's easier for an author to expand their script at a later date than to remove content from their story.

It's important for writers, especially new writers to understand the importance of original story length as it relates to screenwriting. The average script length of 120 pages holds the content of a story written at novella length. The length of the average novella is between 26,000 to 30,000 words.

My advice to authors who want to turn a completed story into a screenplay is to start with an awesome story composed of about 30,000 words and then adapt that novella into a script. You can always add to your story later to turn it into a novel.

Experienced writers can create a story directly in script format.

Principle #2 Keep It Very Simple

There's no need to reinvent the scriptwriting process. There are a few tools to help simplify things.

- **Read Scripts:**

There are a few online sites that allow you to read popular movie and television scripts for free. Analyze how screenwriters structure scripts and tell their stories within that structure.

- **Use Scriptwriting Software:**

If you are on a budget use a template in a Word processing template. However, the great thing about scriptwriting software is that they make formatting a script easy. You click on a scene header command, the heading aligns on the page, you type or paste in the text and each page is properly numbered for you. Later versions of Word also have a screenwriting template, but ensure that you set the margins and font to the correct standard of the entity you are submitting your script to.

- **Length of a Script:**

Script and movie lengths are broken down as follows:
- One page = about one minute.
- A <u>feature screenplay</u> is generally 120 pages or less in length.
- A short film script is usually 60 pages or shorter in length.

Some film competitions will accept scripts between 130 to 150 pages, but those contests are uncommon. **<u>My advice to novice scriptwriters who decide to enter screenwriting contests, stick to the standard of writing 120 pages or less for features or 60 pages or less for short scripts.</u>**

*It is also preferred that a script is written in 12 pitch courier font.

Principle #3 Keep It Relevant

Your script can live or die based on its first ten pages. Think of the first ten pages as the first ten minutes of a movie. You want to hold the interest of movie goers within the first few minutes of the film.

Whoever reads your script is thinking about how your story will play to an audience. I can think of more than a few alleged horror and action movies that delivered nothing but slow dialogue for the first thirty minutes of the film. When I write a horror, action or comedy script I ensure that horror, action or comedy happens within the first ten pages.

The second part of relevance is that whatever happens in the first ten pages of your script needs to be relevant to the rest of story. The first ten pages is a good area to artfully connect a main character to a significant supporting character or hint about the setting.

                         JASE
            Waaaay too much info Dad.

Joseph gets into his vehicle and rolls down the driver's window. He leans his head out of the window.

                    JOSEPH DEAN
            You need to loosen up son.

                         STEVE
            Hey Mr. Dean! My father sends his apologies.
            He wanted to give you a personal tour of the
            upgrades at the Resort, but he had to fly to
            Autumntown Hospital to visit his brother. His
            Foreman **Frank** will take care of you.

                    JOSEPH DEAN
            No problem. I hope his brother will be okay. I'm
            sure the upgrades are fine. Your father has the
            best construction business in the west. Don't tell
            him I said that.

Keep it Relevant: Pacing and Timing

It doesn't matter if you're writing drama, horror, comedy or action a screenwriter needs to be mindful of the pacing and timing of the conflict, scares, comedic and or action elements of the story. We discussed the first ten pages, but properly inserting emotional elements at the right intervals help drive the energy of a story within a limited number of pages.

I saw a movie that had an action sequence about every thirty seconds. It had so much action that it lacked a comprehensive story. As they say, "Too much of a good thing ain't good." Conversely, since my primary go-to is horror, I really take issue with horror films that don't show so much as a scary kitten within the first thirty minutes of a horror movie. Basically, the lack of your primary emotional element will also make a screenplay boring. Dramas also require that suitable moments of conflict occur to prevent a story from becoming boring.

My advice is to read the scripts of hit movies in your genre. Examine the intervals when a screenwriter inserts emotional elements. Note how many pages are between scares, jokes or action sequences. The emotional elements of your storyline won't match the timing of another screenwriter's story, but studying other scripts will help you learn how to properly pace the emotional elements in script format so that you can illicit the correct emotional responses from your audience.

The bottom line is to read scripts to get a feel for pacing and timing. Slowing the emotional element down by one or two pages may be warranted. Don't let script structure constrain your creative storytelling.

In the next section check out how I handled the basics and pacing in my cash award winning dramatic autobiographic feature script, Stronger When She's Broken.

Note: Due to formatting for this book, the screenplay appears longer than the standard feature length, but it is actually 120 pages.

PART FOUR

Multiple Award Winning Screenplay

STRONGER WHEN SHE'S BROKEN: After she's told she is dying, a writer decides to write a story about her courageous journey out of the streets. She learns that the grass isn't always greener in her new life; but with lessons learned from her Old-G father the writer finds triumph. Contains true events, American history, intense drama, mild adult language, brief mild intimacy, violence, humor and TRIUMPH. © 2020

FADE IN:

SUPERIMPOSE OVER BLACK "BASED ON TRUE EVENTS."

EXT. TOPS OF GREEN TREES - DAY

Sunshine peeks through the rustling green
leaves of branches of tall trees.

                    SHALANN (V.O.)
          A significant emotional event.
          That's what experts call a
          situation with a trial so hard
          that it has the power to break
          your very soul. Some people
          never experience a significant
          emotional event, but others
          experience many. You never know
          what you may do when life's
          journey hits you with a series
          of very hard tests. Here's how I
          handled the hard tests on my
          life's journey.

Sound of loud rustling leaves accompanies
scene transition.

INT. DOCTOR'S OFFICE - DAY (PRESENT DAY)

SHALANN, a beautiful Black woman in her mid-
50s sits in a chair across the desk from her
neurologist, DR. FERRY. ShaLann tries not to
fidget with her hands while her doctor thumbs
through a few pages in a manila folder.

                    DR. FERRY
          Hmm? Hmm? Hmm?

                    SHALANN
        Give it to me straight Doc. I
        write horror. I can take it.
        Is my old stroke acting up on
        me again?

The doctor slides a few pages across the desk
to ShaLann.

ShaLann glances over one of the pages.

                    DR. FERRY
        Did you know that you have
        a hole in your heart?
                    SHALANN
             (surprised)

        No.

                    DR. FERRY
        Not only do you have a hole in
        your heart, but you also have
        Lupus.

ShaLann sits there in shock, blankly
starring at the wall behind the doctor's
desk.

                    DR. FERRY (CONT'D)
        Lupus is attacking your cardio
        vascular system. It's not only
        aggravating your old stroke,
        but it's impacting the blood
        flow to your heart too. You're
        looking at having a massive
        heart attack or a major stroke
        any day now.

Her doctor picks up the pages from his desk and then pushes them into a manila folder.

> DR. FERRY (CONT'D)
> I wrote down the number to the local Lupus support group. I also put a referral for a Cardiologist in here.

He reaches out his hand and offers the folder to ShaLann, but she continues to stare ahead.

> DR. FERRY (CONT'D)
> I'm so sorry Ms. Moore, but there's nothing else I can do for you.

ShaLann stares ahead.

> DR. FERRY(CONT'D)
> (raises voice)
> Ms. Moore!

He startles ShaLann out of her moment of shock.

> SHALANN
> Oh. Yes. Thank you. Thank you.

ShaLann takes the folder from his hand.

ShaLann walks to the door. She grabs the door handle then turns towards the doctor.

> SHALANN (CONT'D)
> Thank you.

ShaLann leaves the office.

INT/EXT. SHALANN'S CAR - DAY

ShaLann calls her AUNT JAXX before driving
down the road.

>   AUNT JAXX (V.O.)
>   (through car speaker)
> Hey. I was just about to call
> you. I need to give you my
> Saudi shopping list.

>   SHALANN
> My work in Saudi Arabia is
> over. My doctor just told me
> that I have Lupus and it's
> trying to kill me.

>   AUNT JAXX (V.O.)
>   (through car speaker)
> Oh Jesus no! Are you okay?

>   SHALANN
> Oddly I feel kind of numb.

>   AUNT JAXX (V.O.)
>   (through car speaker)
> It's not over til it's over.

>   SHALANN
> Hey my horror novel just won
> first prize in an international
> book competition.

>   AUNT JAXX (V.O.)
>   (through car speaker)
> Congratulations! Damn! I bet
> your emotions are all over the
> place.

                    SHALANN
          It's weird, but I feel pretty
          numb about all of it. I've
          really been thinking about my
          life's crazy journey.

                    AUNT JAXX (V.O.)
               (through car speaker)
          Maybe you should
          write about it.

                    SHALANN
          About what?

                    AUNT JAXX (V.O.)
               (through car speaker)
          Your life. Maybe a movie
          story like they did for
          what's her name.

                    SHALANN
          I don't know how to write a movie.

                    AUNT JAXX (V.O.)
               (through car speaker)
          You're good at figuring stuff out.

                    SHALANN
          I gotta go.

ShaLann ends the call.

                    SHALANN (V.O.)
          Figure it out? I don't have
          that kind of time.

EXT. FRONT OF SUNSHINE HOSPITAL - DAY

People walk in and out of the front entrance
of the hospital.

INT. OUTSIDE OF MEETING ROOM #1 - DAY

ShaLann shows up for the Lupus Support Group meeting at 11 a.m.

She tries to open the double doors, but both doors are locked.

ShaLann sits on a sofa and waits. She checks her watch and sees that it's twenty minutes later.
ShaLann decides to leave.

INT/EXT. SHALANN'S CAR - DAY

ShaLann calls the head of the Support Group.

                HEAD OF LUPUS GROUP (V.O.)
        (over phone)
    Hello.

                SHALANN
    Hi I'm at the Lupus Support
    Group, but the doors are
    locked. Did you guys switch
    locations?

                HEAD OF LUPUS GROUP
    I'm sorry, but someone was supposed
    to notify all of the group members
    that leader of your group died last
    night.

                SHALANN
    Of what?

                HEAD OF LUPUS GROUP
    Lupus.

ShaLann ends the call.

                    SHALANN (V.O.)
          It was at that moment that
          it all hit me. The terror.
          The heartache. The tears.
          The absolute fricking
          reality of my life.

ShaLann sits in her car and screams. ShaLann screams again and again and again and again.

ShaLann hollers and sobs profusely.

Finally, ShaLann dries her tears and collects

herself.

EXT. DISPENSARY - DAY

ShaLann exits her parked car in front of a Marijuana Dispensary.

INT. SHALANN'S BEDROOM - DAY

ShaLann sits in front of her laptop finishing up a doobie brownie and a couple of shots of Remy Martin on ice.

She stares at the computer screen.

                    SHALANN (V.O.)
          Where should I begin? Oh, I know.

                            DISSOLVE TO:

BEGIN PRIMARY FLASHBACK:

INT/EXT. TAXI CAB - DAY (1986)

Twenty-two-year-old ShaLann stares out of a partially opened rear window during her ride in the backseat of a taxi. She's cute, five-foot-three with a complexion about the tone of ten drops of cream in cup of black coffee.

The hot summer sun beams down on the traffic is stalled due to road construction.

ShaLann looks over at a liquor store.

> SHALANN (V.O.)
> The Hood. It's like a
> prison without walls.
> People are either too
> poor to change it or too
> poor to get out of it.
> It leads to a lot of
> desperation.

Above the traffic noise ShaLann sees and hears two bums argue over a shopping cart.

> SHALANN (V.O.)
> Or despair.

A mentally ill woman walks by the taxi arguing with herself.

> SHALANN (V.O.)
> In the Hood each child
> has to find a way out.

A MAN IN A HAT is walking with a four-year-old little girl wearing a red and blue dress.

The girl cries when she falls and hurts her knee.

> MAN IN A HAT
> Come on. Get up.

The little girl continues to sit on the ground crying.

ShaLann watches the man and daughter. She remembers a similar moment with her father.

BEGIN CHILDHOOD FLASHBACK

EXT. FRONT OF TWO STORY BRICK HOME - DAY (1968)

Five-year-old ShaLann is dressed in a red, white and blue short set to celebrate the 4th of July.

Little ShaLann stands on the lower step in front of her Grandma's house playing with a sparkler.

ShaLann's GRANDMA sits in a chair on the front porch watching her granddaughter play.

ShaLann gets excited when she sees her father's convertible, brown Cadillac park in the driveway.

She jumps off the step and bolts towards the car. She trips on a crack in the sidewalk and falls hard on her left knee.

She cries and screams as blood pores from her wounded knee.

ShaLann sees her father's feet walk toward her. Her father PRINCE PETER reaches out his hand towards her.

                    PRINCE PETER
          Get up Lann.

ShaLann is crying inconsolably. She shakes her head no.

Her father reaches out his hand.

ShaLann's Grandma grows impatient with the scene.
                    SHALANN'S GRANDMA
          Don't let her cry like that!
          Pick her up Pete!

                    PRINCE PETER
          Come on Lann get up. Close
          your eyes real tight and...

END CHILDHOOD FLASHBACK

                              BACK TO SCENE:

INT/EXT. TAXI CAB - DAY (SUMMER 1986)

The TAXI DRIVER looks at ShaLann in his
rearview mirror.

                    TAXI DRIVER
          So you're about to sign up
          and change your life today
          huh?

                    SHALANN
          I'm sorry what?

                    TAXI DRIVER
          I said, you're about to
          sign your name on the
          dotted line and change your
          life today right?

                    SHALANN
          That's my plan man.

                    TAXI DRIVER
          Good! You need to get away
          from these streets. The
          other night these thugs
          shot into the back of my
          cab and blew this cat's
          head clean off. His partner
          got away and skipped out on
          the fare. Crack!

The driver looks in the rearview mirror. He
sees ShaLann looking around the backseat.

                    TAXI DRIVER (CONT'D)
          Don't worry, that was a different
          car. You didn't hear about it?

                    SHALANN
          Yeah I heard about it. Damn shame.

BEGIN FLASHBACK.

INT. BACK DOOR IN SHALANN'S KITCHEN - NIGHT

ShaLann enters her dark kitchen and grabs a
butcher knife from the drawer when she
hears a light knocking at her back door.

ShaLann peeps through the side of the curtain
and sees her Cousin JERSEY. He is very
agitated.

                    JERSEY
          Come on Cuz. Let me in!

ShaLann opens the back door. Jersey rushes
in. ShaLann turns on the kitchen light.

Jersey's hair and upper body are covered
with bloody material.

                    SHALANN
                (whispering)
          Jersey? What's that crap on you?

Jersey is pacing and freaking out.

                    JERSEY
                (raises voice)
          My homeboy's blood,
          brains and bone!

                    SHALANN
          Keep your voice down. You'll
          wake everybody up.

                    JERSEY
                (freaking out)
        We wuz in a cab and these
        dudes pulled up next to us
        and blew my boy's head off.
        Clean off!

                    SHALANN
        What the heck is wrong
        with you bringing that
        crap here? You just put
        our family in danger!

ShaLann peeps out the window in the back door
to see if Jersey has been followed.

                    JERSEY
        I don't think they want
        me. They just looked at
        me and drove off. I need
        to use your phone.

                    SHALANN
        Use the phone and bounce!
        And don't get that mess on
        my phone either! Sloppy
        criminal!

ShaLann hand's him some paper towels and the
kitchen phone.

ShaLann watches Jersey make a call. She closes
the door behind him after he leaves.

ShaLann uses paper napkins from the napkin
holder sitting on the kitchen table to clean
up bits of bone and brain from the floor. She
tosses the dirty napkins into the toilet then
watches the wad of bloody paper swirl in the
flushing water.

END FLASHBACK.

BACK TO SCENE:

INT/EXT. TAXI CAB - DAY (SUMMER 1986)

                    TAXI DRIVER
          Like I said, a nice young
          lady needs to get out of
          these streets.

                    SHALANN
          Hopefully I'm off to a
          better life with green
          pastures covered in milk
          and honey.

                    TAXI DRIVER
          I don't know about all
          that. I'm a Nam vet.

                    SHALANN
          Oh? What branch?

                    TAXI DRIVER
          Army. They messed me up with
          that Agent Orange. You know
          the government still denies
          involvement in that
          nightmare?

                    SHALANN
          That's terrible!

                    TAXI DRIVER
          News flash. Those
          government jack-holes
          did it. They even say
          the military was
          involved in that
          Tuskegee Experiment.

                    SHALANN
          Really?

The taxi stops in front of the military
recruiting station.

                    TAXI DRIVER
          That'll be eight-fifty.

ShaLann gives him ten dollars.

                    SHALAN
          N Keep the
          change.

                    TAXI DRIVER
          Thanks pretty lady!

As ShaLann exits the cab the driver
interrupts ShaLann before she closes the
door.

                    TAXI DRIVER (CONT'D)
          Hey! Here's a tip for
          your tip: Watch out for
          them racist good ole boys
          and whatever you do - The
          driver looks at ShaLann
          with a very serious
          expression.

                    TAXI DRIVER (CONT'D)
          Stay away from Navy experiments.
          Have a blessed life!

                    SHALANN
               (awkward)
          Thank you.

INT. MILITARY RECRUITING STATION - DAY

ShaLann stands in the hallway of the Military Recruiting Office. She stares at four big arrows hanging on a wall.

Three arrows point left towards the Army, Navy and Marines. One arrow points right, towards the Air Force recruiter.
ShaLann looks down at the label on the folder in her hand. The label reads Navy Recruiter.

She looks up at the arrows on the wall again.

ShaLann follows the arrow to the Air Force Recruiter's Office.

                              DISSOLVE TO:

EXT. AIR FORCE BASIC TRAINING (1986) - NIGHT

ShaLann is wearing civilian clothes as she carries her suitcase off of a dark blue military bus. She lines up next to other recruits.

                    SHALANN (V.O)
          I made it to Basic Training
          at Lackland Air Force Base,
          Texas.

A male recruit starts crying.

A couple of Air Force guys wearing Smokey the Bear hats start yelling and pushing over the suitcases of all of the people laughing.

More Drill Sergeants rush over and start yelling and kicking luggage.

                    SHALANN (V.O.)
          All of that crying in
          front of the Smokey the
          Bear hats is a big
          mistake.

A male Drill Sergeant walks up to ShaLann. He
points to his right, indicating for her to
line up with a group of females.

                    SHALANN
               Yes sir!

ShaLann sails through without a problem.

There are no Drill Sergeants standing near
the female recruits.

The women shake their heads as they watch the
Drill Sergeants harass the guys.

A FEMALE RECRUIT #1 whispers to ShaLann.

                    FEMALE RECRUIT #1
          Look at those losers. I
          watched all of the military
          TV shows so I'm fully
          prepared for this crap.

                    SHALANN
          Me too. What a bunch of Gomers.

                    WHITE FEMALE RECRUIT #2
          My father was in the Army. He
          told me everything that I need to
          do. This should be a cake walk.

                    SHALANN (V.O.)
          My father was in the Army too.
          His stint in the Army was no
          cake walk.

BEGIN FLASHBACK

EXT. ARMY CAMP NORTH KOREA - DAY (1954)

> SHALANN (V.O.)
> Let me tell you a little bit
> about my father Prince
> Peter.
>
> At the age of sixteen, he
> earned his place in the
> history books as one of the
> first groups of negroes
> integrated into the U.S. Army
> during the Korean War.

An image of a newspaper with the headline
"PRESIDENT TRUMAN WIPES OUT SEGREGATION IN
ARMED FORCES" appears on the screen then
disappears two seconds later.

Prince Peter, a sixteen-year-old, tall medium
brown skinned soldier unloads a large bag of
potatoes from the rear of a large Army pickup
truck.

An angry White ARMY CAPTAIN notices Peter
unloading the truck and stomps towards him.

> ARMY CAPTAIN
> (to Prince Peter)
> What the frack are you doing boy?

Peter jumps down from the back of the truck.
He stands erect at the position of attention.

> PRINCE PETER
> Unloading potatoes - sir.

                    ARMY CAPTAIN
          I told you to have all of these
          sacks unloaded a half hour ago!

Peter relaxes his posture. He is expressionless
when he looks the officer in his eyes.

                    PRINCE PETER
          The cooks asked me to slow down
          until they cleared more storage
          room. They don't want them on the
          ground near the rats and bugs
          sir.

The officer points his finger in Peter's face.

                    ARMY CAPTAIN
          I don't give a frack nig-
          gro! All of you negroes are
          worthless. I don't know why
          they let you in the Ar...

Before the Captain could finish his sentence
Prince Peter punches him in the nose, which
knocks the officer to the ground. Peter jumps on
top of the officer and pummels him in the face
with a barrage of punches.

Prince Peter is wild eyed as he tries to pry
the officer's mouth open. He grabs the
officers chin with one hand and his cheeks
with the other.

Other soldiers rush to the scene. They try to
pull Peter off of the officer.

                    PRINCE PETER
          Open up honkey so I can
          snatch that foul tongue out
          of your mutha-frickin'
          mouth. Open up cracker! Open
          that nasty mouth up!

Peter dislocates the officer's jaw.

Other soldiers pull Peter off of the officer.

The officer lays on the ground moaning and bleeding with his lower jaw crooked in an unnatural position.

Several soldiers hold Peter back as he struggles to break free to go after the injured Captain again.

END FLASHBACK

                    SHALANN (V.O.)
          Let's hope my military
          journey turns out better
          than my father's.
                              DISSOLVE TO:

EXT. AIR FORCE BASIC TRAINING - DAY

The troops tend to do things in squads of sixteen, four per row with the shortest recruits in last row. ShaLann always ends up in the last row.

BEGIN BASIC TRAINING MONTAGE:

                    SHALANN (V.O.)
          In Basic we do a lot of running...

ShaLann wears grey sweats as she runs in the back row of a squad of recruits, with four in each row.

EXT. BASIC TRAINING FIELD - DAY

                    SHALANN (V.O.) CONT.
          And marching...

ShaLann wears an olive green fatigue uniform as she marches in a group of female Airmen.

EXT. BASIC TRAINING FIELD - DAY

                    SHALANN (V.O.)
          And standing around like
          good little soldiers.

ShaLann and other recruits dressed in their fatigues stand erect and quiet, with their arms placed tightly by their sides.

END BASIC TRAINING MONTAGE.

INT. CHOW HALL - DAY

                    SHALANN (V.O.)
          The biggest part of
          Basic is the constant
          yelling.

Male and female recruits stand in the serving line to get their breakfast.

ShaLann stands between two male recruits. An ASIAN TEXAN AIRMAN stands on her left and a tall guy, BOSTON AIRMAN stands on her right.

                    SHALANN
          I'd like eggs, bacon grits and...

Sam the Asian Texan Airman interrupts her.

                    ASIAN TEXAN AIRMAN
          You gettin' too much food.

                    SHALANN
          What?

                    BOSTON AIRMAN
          You won't have time to
          eat it.

                    SHALANN
          Why?

                    ASIAN TEXAN AIRMAN
          And don't sit close to the
          trash cans either.

                    SHALANN
          Wait. What?

                    BOSTON AIRMAN
          We warned you.

The Boston Airman and the Asian Texan Airman
rush to their seats.

All of the recruits sit down and begin to eat.

ShaLann watches the two guys scarf down their
food like they're trying to win an eating
contest.

All of a sudden a GROUP OF DRILL SERGEANTS
start yelling in the faces of all of the
recruits. Their voices sound like they are
coming from everywhere.

                    GROUP OF DRILL SERGEANTS
                    (yelling)
          Smell it and get up! You ain't
          got that kind of time! Smell it
          and get up!

Drill sergeants slide big black trash cans to
the end of each table.

Recruits begin standing up and heading towards
the food disposal line.

>   GROUP OF DRILL SERGEANTS
>   (yelling)
>   Toss that food in the
>   trashcan at the end of
>   your table!

Airmen scramble to comply.

>   GROUP OF DRILL SERGEANTS
>   (yelling)
>   Smell it and get up! You
>   ain't got that kind of
>   time!

ShaLann fills out her right cheek with bacon
and eggs as she slowly walks towards a trash
can.

>   DISSOLVE TO:

INT. LATRINE IN FEMALE BARRACKS - NIGHT

>   SHALANN (V.O.) CONT.
>   When we're not marching or
>   getting yelled at we're
>   somewhere frickin cleaning.

ShaLann is on her knees scrubbing behind a
toilet with a long handled brush.

ShaLann wipes off a mirror in the latrine
while someone is taking a loud fart filled
crap in the toilet behind her.

ShaLann covers her nose with her hand.

The pooping VALLEY GIRL AIRMAN speaks in
Valley Girl jargon from behind the closed door
of a toilet stall.

                    VALLEY GIRL AIRMAN
              Sorry to do this to ya. That
              chow hall grindage is totally
              gnarley. Pass me a new roll bud-
              dee.

ShaLann hands the Valley Girl Airman a roll
of toilet under the lower opening of the door
to the stall.

                    SHALAN
              N Here ya go.

                    VALLEY GIRL AIRMAN
              Righteous, thanks!
                                      DISSOLVE TO:
EXT. FIELD ON BASE - DAY
ShaLann and her all female squadron stand in
formation at attention. They are wearing an
olive green hat and fatigues.

ShaLann stands in the back row with the
shortest troops. Her buddies Airman GIBSON, a
young white chick from New York stands on her
left and Airman JONES, a young Black chick
from Ohio stands on her right.

                    SHALANN (V.O.)
              It's been a few weeks, but
              the Drill Sergeants still
              get on us for petty crap.

A female drill Sergeant yells in ShaLann's ear
while she is standing at attention.

                    FEMALE DRILL SERGEANT
              There's a frickin' quarter inch
              thread hanging from the back of
              your hat Airman Moore! You
              better frickin' pay attention
              to frickin' detail or that's
              your frickin' butt!

ShaLann remains cool headed as she shouts her
response.

                    SHALANN
          Ma'am yes ma'am!

The female Drill Sergeant rushes towards the
front row when she hears an Airman crying.

ShaLann and the Airmen standing on each side
of her, Airman JONES and Airman GIBSON barely
move their lips as they whisper to each other.

                    JONES
          It's the crying girl again.

                    GIBSON
          It's been weeks now. How
          many tears does that
          chick have?

Another Drill Sergeant leads a group of eight
people past ShaLann's squad. Some of the
Airman are in green fatigues, but some are in
civilian clothes.

                    SHALANN
          What's up with that group?

                    GIBSON
          Casual Squadron.

                    JONES
          It's the sick, injured and
          loonie birds that wash out
          of Basic.

                    SHALANN
          Damn!

                              DISSOLVE TO:

INT. FEMALE BARRACKS - NIGHT

ShaLann and Jones are casually dressed in a
white, short sleeve t-shirt and olive green
fatigue pants. They sit on the floor polishing
their combat boots.

Gibson plops down on the floor next to them.

                    GIBSON
          Man my bunk buddy is working
          my last nerve! I swear if
          she sits on my bunk again
          I'm going to throat punch
          her.

                    SHALANN
          Don't let her rock you
          Gibson. We have another
          week in this place. You
          can't let these chicks get
          you worked up and washed
          out.

                    GIBSON
          Yeah I know. I know. They
          need to give us a meditation
          class while we're in here to
          deal with these chicks.

                    SHALANN
          You ain't never lied. It's
          taking everything in me not
          to bend my cryin' bunk
          buddy's head back.

                    GIBSON
          That's right the crying
          girl is your bunk buddy.

                    JONES
You mean was her bunk buddy.
She got washed out today
because she tried to kill
herself.

                    GIBSON
That's crazy!

                    SHALANN
Yeah, I had to get help
after I found her slitting
her wrist with a sewing
needle.

                    JONES
Word?

                    SHALANN
Word! She said that she was
home sick and wanted out of
here.

                    JONES
Wow! I don't know what kind
of lollipop land that
crying girl came from. I
had to leave before I
killed my evil stepfather.

                    SHALANN
I heard that!

BEGIN CHILDHOOD FLASHBACK

INT. KITCHEN AT AUNT'S HOUSE - DAY (1971)

Ten-year-old ShaLann sits in her forty-year-
old AUNT DORIE's kitchen telling her aunt
about years of abuse at the hands of her
Stepfather.

                        AUNT DORIE
            Y'all act like I can't
            see that somethin's
            wrong, but I know it.
            What's really going on at
            your house.

                        LITTLE SHALANN
            Vanden is evil. He comes
            into my room and...

BEGIN CHILDHOOD MEMORIES

INT. NINE-YEAR-OLD SHALANN'S BEDROOM - DAY

Little ShaLann is sitting on her bed playing
with two green plastic army soldiers when her
stepfather VANDEN enters her room.

                        VANDEN
            Did you turn on the TV?

                        NINE-YEAR-OLD SHALANN
            No.

Vanden becomes enraged!

                        VANDEN
            I know you did it!

Little ShaLann gets up to leave, but Vanden
stops her with a slap so hard that it flings
ShaLann towards a wall.

ShaLann unnaturally bends the tip of her right
pinky finger trying prevent her head from
hitting the wall.

After the beating ShaLann sits on her bed
silently crying as she holds her dislocated
finger. Her four-year-old sister comes into
her bedroom.

                    SHALANN'S LITTLE SISTER
          I'm sorry. I turned on our TV show.
          Don't be mad at me and my daddy.

INT. NINE-YEAR-OLD SHALANN'S BEDROOM - NIGHT

Little ShaLann pretends to be asleep in her
bed. Vanden is drinking a short glass of booze
when he enters her bedroom.

He stares at Little ShaLann while he rubs his
crotch. He steps towards Little ShaLann's bed.

END MEMORIES

                    AUNT DORIE
               (angry)
          I knew some mutha-sucka
          would take advantage of my
          schizophrenic sister! I'm
          calling your Daddy!

ShaLann is so shocked that her Aunt is calling
her father that her mouth drops open.

ShaLann leaves her Aunt's house while she's
still on the phone.

INT. SHALANN'S FATHER'S APARTMENT - DAY

                    SHALANN (V.O.)
          Let me tell you a little
          more about my father. After
          leaving the Army he became
          the notorious Midwest
          gangster, Prince Peter.

INT. PRINCE PETER'S PENTHOUSE - DAY (1968)

ShaLann's father, Prince Peter opens his front
door and sees ten-year-old ShaLann standing
there.

ShaLann looks up at her tall, thirty-year-old
father.

                    SHALANN (V.O.)
          My father Prince Peter.
          He's a notorious Midwestern
          gangster who insists that I
          behave and speak like a
          proper princess.

ShaLann walks into the living room of her
father's apartment.

Two Black men wearing three quarter length
leather jackets, close their coats to hide
their guns when they see little ShaLann.

The two men exit the apartment.

Her father closes the door.

LIVINGROOM

Prince Peter walks into the living room and
sits in the center of a cheetah fur sofa
positioned against a wall in his living room.

A chess game sits on top of a wood and marble
coffee table.

Little ShaLann sits on a Cheetah fur stool on
the other side of the coffee table, across
from her father.

                    PRINCE PETER
          Have a seat on the couch.

Her father sets up a chess game.

                    PRINCE PETER (CONT'D)
          You up for a game of chess?

                    SHALAN
          N Yes Father.

Her father moves a pawn on his right. ShaLann
moves a knight on her right. They slowly play
chess as they talk.

                    SHALANN (CONT'D)
          Did Aunt Dorie call you?

                    PRINCE PETER
          Yes, she did. Remember when
          I taught you how to play
          chess?

                    SHALANN
          Yes.

                    PRINCE PETER
          What did I tell you about
          the most important piece?

                    SHALANN
          Protect the queen at all times.

                    PRINCE PETER
          That's right. What I want
          to know is why didn't you
          tell me about someone
          hurting the queen?

                    SHALANN
          Because I knew that you
          would kill Vanden.

                    PRINCE PETER
          Don't you want him killed?

                    SHALANN
          Well I doooo and I don't.

                    PRINCE PETER
          You're old enough to make a
          decision about this so
          what's the problem?

Her father moves a pawn on his left.

                    SHALANN
          If Vanden is killed it
          will really hurt my
          little sister.

ShaLann moves a pawn on her right.

                    PRINCE PETER
          I see. Well the power over
          Vanden's life is on your
          tongue.

Ten-year-old ShaLann looks at her father.

                    SHALANN
          If it was any other dude
          I'd say kill him, but I
          don't want to hurt my
          sister like that.

                    PRINCE PETER
          Okay, but I'm gonna make
          sure that he never puts his
          hands on another child
          again. Nobody messes with my
          family. Nobody!

                    SHALANN
          Thank you Father.

                    PRINCE PETER
          In the future, you come to
          me if anybody messes with
          you.

                    SHALAN
          N Yes Father.

Prince Peter shows ShaLann a small gun.

                    PRINCE PETER
          In the meantime, take my .22.

                    SHALANN
          Thanks, but I think
          I'll be okay.

Prince Peter pulls a small red pocket knife
from his pocket then gives it to ShaLann.

                    PRINCE PETER
          Take this little pocket
          knife. It doesn't have
          to be big, just stuck
          in the right spots.

ShaLann puts the knife in her right pants
pocket.

                    PRINCE PETER (CONT'D)
          Now let's go get a cheeseburger
          and a milkshake.

                    SHALANN
          Yes. Thank you Father.

END CHILDHOOD FLASHBACK.

                              BACK TO SCENE:

INT. FEMALE BARRACKS - NIGHT

                    SHALANN
          There's no way I'm going
          back to where I came from.

                    GIBSON
          Word! I heard that another
          girl got washed out
          because she got too sick
          from the shots. That's why
          I carry Tylenol in a
          plastic bag in my bra. You
          gotta check that fever
          before the sun makes it
          worse.

                    SHALANN
          Word up on that Tylenol
          trick! I'm not getting
          washed out over some
          bullcrap like being homesick
          or some damn shots.

                    JONES
          Word!

                                   DISSOLVE TO:

EXT. IMMNIZATIONS AT MEDICAL TENT - DAY

ShaLann and other troops wear a white t-shirt
and fatigue bottoms while they wait in the
immunization line.

One by one the Med Tech pushes a cocktail of
vaccines into their left shoulder with a
needless air gun.

The drugs come out with such force that it
causes blood to trickle from ShaLann's
shoulder.

The troops are ordered to sit on the ground
after they get their shot.

ShaLann and her buddies make sure no one is
looking before they pull the Tylenol from
their bras and pop them to stave off a vaccine
fever.

                                    DISSOLVE TO:
INT. MILITARY CLASSROOM - DAY
ShaLann and a mix of male and female airmen
sit in a dimly lit room watching a slide show
of people performing different Air Force jobs.
A Sergeant stands next to the movie screen
giving a description of each job.

                    SHALANN (V.O.)
               Basic Training is almost over.
               Thankfully the yelling stopped.
               I guess that we're at a point
               where we've stopped making
               rookie mistakes. It's also at
               this point where those of us
               who haven't been assigned a
               career field get to pick one.

An image of a woman wearing a blue blazer and
holding a clipboard appears on the screen.

ShaLann raises her hand.

                    SHALANN
               Excuse me Sergeant. Is the
               woman holding the clipboard
               doing an Air Force job?

                    SERGEANT INSTRUCTOR
          Yes. That's a Recreation
          and Club Manager. People in
          that position organize
          parties, events and
          sometimes tours for troop
          morale. You want that job?

                    SHALANN
               (excited)
          Sir, yes sir!

                    SERGEANT INSTRUCTOR
          You got it.

ShaLann cracks a wide closed mouth smile.

                                        DISSOLVE TO:

EXT. HULL OF COMMERCIAL AIRPLANE - DAY
A commercial airplane ascends as it carries
ShaLann away from Basic training. The plane
lands at the Denver Airport.

                    SHALANN (V.O.)
          Bye-bye Basic Training.
          Hello real Air Force heaven.
                                        DISSOLVE TO:

INT. SHALANN'S DORMROOM - NIGHT (1987)

                    SHALANN (V.O.)
          I made it to my first base.
          I have a roommate named
          Penny. She's a Black farm
          girl from Alabama.

PENNY is asleep in her bed.

ShaLann lays in her own bed with her fingers laced behind her head. ShaLann listens to music on her Walkman cassette player.

ShaLann pulls off her headphones when she hears loud music coming from the hallway. She then hears someone knocking hard at her door.

ShaLann is annoyed by the disturbance. She yanks the door open.

Loud music pours in from the hall.

A shirtless young man dressed in Hawaiian shorts, MARTINEZ and a guy holding an empty large bowl, AIRMAN CAMPBELL are standing at the door.

The two Airmen at the door are clearly drunk.

> SHALANN
> Can I help you?

The Airman holding the bowl yells to his friends in the hall.

> AIRMAN CAMPBELL
> Hey! Hey! Turn the music
> down so I can hear!

Penny gets out of bed and rushes to the door in her pajamas.

> PENNY
> What's all this noise?

> AIRMAN CAMPBELL
> Hello, hi, I'm your neighbor,
> Randy Campbell and this is
> Martinez. He's a Crew Chief
> who makes sure that I get the
> best seat when I fly.

                    MARTINEZ
          Hello.

                    SHALANN
          What's up? We're trying to sleep.

                    CAMPBELL
          We want see if we can borrow
          some chips and invite you
          ladies to the hall par-tay.

ShaLann looks into the hall and sees a raging
party with lots of people drinking. Dudes are
belly surfing on a long Slip n Slide.

A shirtless guy wearing Groucho Marx glasses
yells to the guys standing in ShaLann's
doorway.

                    GROUCHO MARX
          AIRMAN
          Are they giving up the chips?
          I clocked them carrying chips
          in a Commissary bag a few
          hours ago.

ShaLann and Penny step into the hall.

                    SHALANN AND PENNY
              (yell in unison)
          And?

                    PENNY
          What you gone get is the cops
          called on you if you don't
          hush up all this noise!

PARTY BOYS in the hall throw their hands in
the air.

                    PARTY BOYS
                  (in unison)
               We are the cops!

Penny yells to herself as she storms back to
bed.

                      PENNY
             Oh good Lord! I'm livin' in
             frickin Animal House! Do they
             even live in this building?

ShaLann steps into the hall in her pajamas.
She closes the door behind her.

                    SHALANN
             Look I'll give you the
             chips if you promise to
             keep the music down.

                 AIRMAN CAMPBELL
             Okay. Hey you want some
             Jungle Juice? My boy just
             made it in his tub so it's
             fresh.

                    SHALANN
             No. I'm not going to drink
             bathtub booze with a bunch of
             strange dudes. That's how crap
             happens.

                 AIRMAN CAMPBELL
             Lady as fine as you are, you
             can walk down this hallway
             naked and ain't nobody gonna
             touch you unless you want them
             to. We family. Anybody gets out
             of pocket like that with
             family, will get a straight up
             beat down.

                    SHALANN
          Cool, but I have to work in the
          morning.

                    AIRMAN CAMPBELL
          On a Saturday?

                    SHALANN
          Yeah I work at the Club.

                    AIRMAN CAMPBELL
          Cool.

ShaLann ducks into her room, grabs a large bag
of chips and gives them to the Airman at the
door.
                    AIRMAN CAMPBELL (CONT'D)
          Thanks! We'll pay you back.
ShaLann closes her door and gets back in bed.
She hears Airman Campbell shout in the hall.

                    AIRMAN CAMPBELL(CONT'D)
          I got the chips!

                    PARTY BOYS
          Woooooooo!

The music rages loud in the hall again.

ShaLann angrily covers her head with her
pillow.
                                        DISSOLVE TO:

EXT. GREY VAN PARKED IN RED ZONE - DAY

ShaLann is getting in a grey passenger van
that she accidentally illegally parked when
two cops pull up in a patrol vehicle. She
doesn't recognize the cops in the car. The
driver, AIRMAN COP smiles and tosses her a
greeting.

                    AIRMAN COP
          Hey Moore.

ShaLann waves to the cops.

                    SHALANN
          Hey guys.

The cops drive away.

                    SHALANN (V.O.)
          The cops are paying me back for
          the party snacks big time.
                                   DISSOLVE TO:

INT. MILITARY BAR - NIGHT

                    SHALANN (V.O.)
          I've gotten into the groove
          at my job too.

BEGIN MONTAGE OF THREE MILITARY BAR SCENES:

1. ShaLann holds a clipboard while standing
behind a bar during hard rock night at the
Club. Guys in military uniform play air guitar
near the bar. A male Bartender looks at
ShaLann and then points to a tap of beer as he
silently mouths...more beer.

ShaLann annotates four next to kegs on the
order sheet that she's holding.

ShaLann looks at the bartender and gives him a
thumbs up.

2. ShaLann holds a clipboard behind a bar
during soul night at the Club. Guys in
military uniform perform a short Pop Lock
dance near the bar.

A male Bartender looks at ShaLann and then holds up an empty bottle of Rum as he silently mouths...more Rum.

ShaLann annotates one case next to rum on her order sheet.

ShaLann looks at the bartender and gives him a thumbs up.

3. ShaLann holds a clipboard behind a bar during a party for Officers. Officers are wearing their dress blues and bow ties near the bar. A male Bartender is making martinis for two male Captains. The bartender looks at ShaLann as he holds up an empty jar of olives as he mouths...more olives. He and the two Captains stare at ShaLann.

ShaLann grabs a bar-back and whispers in his ear to get more olives STAT! The bar-back trots to the back and rushes over to the bartender with a jar of olives.

The bartender drops an olive in each martini.

                    SHALANN
          Sorry about that Captains.

One CAPTAIN CUSTOMER takes a sip of his drink. He turns to ShaLann.

                    CAPTAIN-CUSTOMER
          Don't let it happen again.

The two Captains walk away.

ShaLann gives the bartender a look of relief before giving him a thumbs up.

END MONTAGE.

                    SHALANN (V.O.)
          Look at me doin' my Air Force
          thang! I'm actually getting
          paid to organize parties and
          shopping trips. This is a
          military job that I'm a
          downright expert at.

                              DISSOLVE TO:

EXT. STEAMBOAT SPRINGS SKI RESORT - DAY

ShaLann and BREENY stand outside of the tour
bus. They watch people exit the bus and walk
towards the ski rental building.

                    SHALANN
          Have fun everyone.

ShaLann smiles and waves to the tour group.

                    BREENY
          Hey ShaLann, I heard a rumor
          that we're supposed to start
          war skills training.

                    SHALANN
          Why? We're not at war.

                    BREENY
          Maybe President Reagan knows
          something we don't know.

                    SHALANN
          Stop being ridiculous. It's not
          like Reagan can predict who the
          next president will be or that
          the new guy will get us
          involved in a war.

                    BREENY
          We shouldn't take this stuff
          too serious. Like they would
          ever put us Club folks in a
          dangerous situation anyway.

                    SHALANN
          Right.
                                        DISSOLVE TO:

INT. TRAINING IN LARGE BASE GYMNASIUM - DAY

ShaLann, Breeny and eight other Airmen scrunch
their faces and cover their noses at the smell
of rotting flesh as they stand just inside of
the entrance of the gym.

A line of light grey room dividers block
ShaLann and the other Airmen from seeing
what's happening in the gym.

ShaLann and the other Airmen can only hear
voices of people screaming, moaning in pain
and shouts of help me.

Some of the Airmen shudder when they hear loud
sounds of a bad recording of gunshots and
explosions.

                    MALE AIRMAN
          Did you guys smell that stench
          outside? Death smells and war
          sounds. Dude they're really
          trying to mess with our heads.

                    SHALANN
          I still smell it. It's like
          someone rubbed essence of dead
          rotting rats all over the
          building.

                    FEMALE AIRMAN #3
          I heard that they hung pieces
          of raw chicken in the trees a
          few days ago so that they could
          totally gross us out.

                    FEMALE AIRMAN #4
          I'm already trying not to toss
          my cookies from my last round
          of shots. This funk ain't
          helping.

                    FEMALE AIRMAN #3
          Like, seriously me too. That
          Typhoid shot was the worse.

                    SHALANN
          Seriously, for real!

                    BREENY
          My Grandfather said the
          government tried to turn guys
          into super soldiers just like
          in the comics. I hope I get a
          super brain so I can levitate
          stuff.

ShaLann and the other Airmen give Breeny a
concerned side eye while they ponder what he
said.

ShaLann and her group are interrupted when an
Air Force Staff Sergeant, MILITARY TRAINER
TALLEY squeezes between two partitions and
walks towards them.

Breeny whispers to ShaLann.

                    BREENY (CONT'D)
          Hey that's the guy from the Chow
          Hall.
                    MILITARY TRAINER TALLEY
          Listen up. I'm Sergeant Talley
          from the Food Service Section.
          I will be your trainer today.
          This is a realistic exercise
          so maintain a military bearing
          of professionalism.

Military Trainer Talley uses an open hand to
point to the room dividers.

                    MILITARY TRAINER TALLEY
          Beyond this point you will see a
          simulation of the aftermath of an
          aircraft crash near a battlefield.
          People are wearing moo-lahge makeup
          to make them appear severely
          injured so do not freak out!

          Your job is to condition yourself to
          block out the mayhem while you
          attend to the deceased. Again,
          maintain your military bearing
          because our team   is being
          graded. Now follow me.

Breeny is walking directly behind ShaLann. He
leans close to whisper to her.

                    BREENY
          Dead bodies? The only dead meat
          I want to deal with is a medium
          well steak.

ShaLann shushes Breeny.

The military instructor pushes one of the
dividers to the side.

ShaLann and the other Airmen can see people
laying on mats that are sprinkled throughout
most of the gym.

Sergeants with clip boards walk around
documenting things that they observe.

The people laying on the floor are made up to
look like something out of a gory horror movie.

Some people are moaning and groaning while
holding fake arms or fake feet. Some have
their real limbs hidden under fake blood
stained clothing as if their limbs are
missing.

The worst makeup effects are the fake injuries
on people's faces. A few people have fake
eyeballs laying on their cheeks. Some look
like they have part of their noses and jaws
missing.

                    MILITARY TRAINER TALLEY
          Watch your step in here. There
          are fake limbs scattered
          everywhere.
ShaLann and the other Airmen in the group step
over fake body parts laying on the floor.

                    BREENY
          (whispers loudly)
          Oh my god this scene is so
          realistic! I'm grossed out to
          the max! I think I'm going to
          spew chunks.

                    SHALANN
                (whispers loudly)
        Keep your crap together Breeny!
        The Commander will make us work
        twelve hour shifts if we
        embarrass the squadron.

As the group follows the instructor, a few of
the Airmen continue to shudder each time they
hear a fake bomb go off.

The military trainer leads ShaLann's group to
an office that has been converted to look like
a medical examination room.

A dummy is laying on a table in a partially
zipped black body bag.

Another Staff Sergeant sits on a stool in a
corner of the room holding a clip board.

                    MILITARY TRAINER TALLEY
                Alright people, the clubs and
                food service fields are
                responsible for keeping meats
                refrigerated on base. Well when
                we're out in the field we also
                have to keep human remains
                refrigerated.

                    BREENY
                What? We'll have to keep body
                parts next to the food?

                    MILITARY TRAINER TALLEY
                No. Remains will be kept in a
                separate refrigeration unit. Today
                you will practice properly
                labeling and storing large and
                small remains.

Sergeant Talley rests his hand on the shoulder
of the dummy laying in the body bag.

> MILITARY TRAINER TALLEY
> Dead bodies are very heavy so
> lift with your legs.

Sergeant Talley looks over at ShaLann and
three females standing next to her.

> MILITARY TRAINER TALLEY
> Except for you cuties. The
> guys will do the heavy lifting.

ShaLann and three female Airmen muster a fake
smile and a giggle.

> SHALANN (V.O.)
> Oh that's frickin hilarious!
> Women have to be strong enough
> to take war like a man and
> smart enough not to hurt the
> egos of the sexist men in
> charge.

Sgt. Talley unzips the body bag to reveal the
naked feet of the dummy laying on the table.

He demonstrates on the dummy as he speaks.

> MILITARY TRAINER TALLEY
> This will include hand and foot
> printing of the deceased. If the
> deceased does not have hands or
> feet, but there is a head
> attached, document what you've
> found on this card, place the
> documents in one of these
> plastic pouches and place in the
> body bag with the deceased like
> so and zip up the bag.

                    BREENY
        I guess you flip em and zip em.
        Haha! You know flip pancakes.

Airman Breeny and a few other airmen laugh.

ShaLann notices the Sergeant who is observing
the group shoot Breeny a dirty look before
scribbling a long note on his clipboard.

ShaLann looks agitated as she side-eyes Breeny.

                              DISSOLVE TO:

INT. DANCE FLOOR AT MILITARY CLUB - MORNING

ShaLann and the Airmen from her training group
sit in chairs near the dance floor of the
otherwise empty closed club.

A military guy with a mustache walks into the
bar area. ShaLann recognizes SERGEANT GRUNDLE.

                    SERGEANT GRUNDLE
        Good Morning. Most of you
        know me from the front
        office. I'm Sergeant Brad
        Grundle. After your
        unprofessional behavior at a
        major training event I've
        been sent over here to whip
        you guys into shape.

                    SHALANN (V.O.)
        That darn goofy Breeny got us
        all screwed! Now we have to
        deal with a guy rumored to be
        one of the biggest jack-holes
        on base.

                    SERGEANT GRUNDLE
          Starting tomorrow you are
          all on twelve hour shifts
          for the next month.

Collective groans of discontent and whining
echo from the group. AIRMAN COLE and AIRMAN #1
are voice their concerns.

                    AIRMAN COLE (FEMALE)
          I got finals this week.

                    AIRMAN #1 (MALE)
          What am I supposed to do
          about my kid?

                    SERGEANT GRUNDLE
          Tough frickin' cookies!

Sergeant Grundle runs his finger across the
top of the bar.

                    SERGEANT GRUNDLE (CONT'D)
          I want this place cleaned from top
          to bottom both inside and outside.
          When you're done with the Club,
          you'll clean all three gyms, Arts
          and Crafts and the Rec Center.

                    SHALANNN (V.O.)
          Welp, it looks like the joy
          ride is over.

                              DISSOLVE TO:

INT. POOL TABLE AREA OF AIRMAN'S CLUB - DAY

ShaLann, Breeny and Airman Cole are cleaning
fluorescent light fixtures and dusting at the
Club.

AIRMAN COLE

Thanks Breeny! Your clown show
got us all screwed. Now we have
to deal with that megalomaniac.
Even the cops on base hate the
guy. I guarantee you they're
going to start riding us because
of him.

BREENY

It's only for a week.

AIRMAN COLE

He said that we will be on
twelves for a month, but he's
going to be here longer.

SHALANN

I've only heard rumors about
the guy. Is he really that
bad?

AIRMAN COLE

That dude has been in since
the sixties. He still has
that backwards way of
thinking.

SHALAN

N That's not
good.

AIRMAN COLE

Let me put it this way, if
Attila the Hun and Archie
Bunker could produce a child
it would grow up to be
Sergeant Grundle.

DISSOLVE TO:

INT. OFFICE AREA IN AIRMAN'S CLUB - DAY

ShaLann, Cole and Breeny share desks in an open office.

ShaLann and Airman Cole sit at their desks doing paperwork. Rhonda, the office secretary rushes through the door and stands next to the doorway in an attempt to hide from someone in the hall.

As soon as Sergeant Grundle walks into the office Airman Cole gets up and leaves the office.

Sergeant Grundle grabs Rhonda by the back of her neck and bends her upper body onto ShaLann's desk.

ShaLann is face to face with Rhonda who is crying in fear.

                    SERGEANT GRUNDLE
          You don't pull away from me!

Sergeant Grundle squeezes Rhonda's butt and rubs his hand between her legs.

                    SERGEANT GRUNDLE (CONT'D)
          You're not going to say
          anything are you Airman Moore?

ShaLann sits in her chair staring at Grundle and Rhonda's mouth is partially gaped open in shock.

Sergeant Grundle releases Rhonda and she runs out of the office in tears.

Grundle turns to ShaLann.

                    SERGEANT GRUNDLE (CONT'D)
          I need for you to get fifty
          dollars in petty cash from
          Charlotte Hescher for office
          supplies. And don't let her
          Jew you down to a lesser
          amount.

ShaLann has an angry look on her face.

                    SHALANN
          Yes.
                    SERGEANT GRUNDLE
          Don't look at me with that
          attitude you frickin' Black
          heffa! Now go get that petty
          cash.

                    SHALANN
          Yes Sergeant Grundle.

ShaLann walks out of the office.

EXT. PARKING LOT OF BASE EXCHANGE - DAY

ShaLann returns to the van and finds a ticket on
the windshield. She looks at the ticket. The van
has been cited for its rear tire sitting on the
parking space line.
                    SHALANN (V.O.)
          Damn! Cole was right! The
          cops are on us for petty
          crap.

                              DISSOLVE TO:
INT. POOL TABLE AREA - DAY

ShaLann, Breeny and Cole wait for Sergeant
Grundle.

Rhonda enters via the door in the pool table
area carrying an arm full of files.
Sergeant Grundle rushes over to help RHONDA.

                    SERGEANT
          GRUNDLE Hey, let me help
          you with that.

                    RHONDA
          That's okay. I got it.

Sergeant Grundle proceeds to pull the folders
from Rhonda's arms. He brushes her right
breast with the palm of his right hand.

Breeny and Cole quickly look away. They bend
down and pretend to tie their boots.

                    SERGEANT
          GRUNDLE Sorry I brushed
          your boob. Feels like
          you've been working out.

ShaLann stares at the two of them with concern.

INT. SHALANN'S DORMROOM - NIGHT

Penny and ShaLann sit on their individual
beds as they talk.

                    SHALANN
          Penny a few of us are
          going to The Rock Island.
          You wanna go?

                    PENNY
          I don't know about going to
          an island at night. Are
          y'all taking a boat?

                    SHALANN
          Nawl country bumpkin. This
          city is land locked. It's a
          dance club. Come on. Let's go
          to a disco.

INT. THE ROCK ISLAND DANCE CLUB - NIGHT

The Rock Island is a huge dance club that
plays 80's pop and new wave music.

An "L" shaped ensemble of high-low dance
platforms line half of the dance floor.

ShaLann and Penny order drinks from a BARTENDER.

                    BARTENDER
          What can I get you ladies?

                    SHALANN
          I'll have a cognac with a splash of
          seven and a coke with cherries for
          my designated driver.

ShaLann and Penny sip their drinks while they
watch people dance.

ShaLann sees a familiar Black lady dancing on
a riser. ShaLann waves to get her attention.

                    SHALANN (CONT'D)
          Hey, look it's Nessa.

NESSA waves back. She walks over and joins
ShaLann and Penny at the bar.

ShaLann sits on a stool between her friends.

                    NESSA
          Bartender may I have a water
          please.

                    SHALANN
          Nessa this is my roommate
          Penny. Penny, Nessa. Her
          mother, works at my job.

                    PENNY
          Nice to meet you.

                    NESSA
          Likewise; speaking of my mom,
          somebody needs to do something
          about that Grundle dude on
          your job. That butt-head
          called my mom a dumb broad!

                    PENNY
          What?

                    SHALANN
          Girl the dude is working my
          last nerve. Frickin' Black
          heffa is his new nick name
          for me.

                    PENNY
          What?

                    NESSA
          He better watch his mouth
          before somebody knocks his
          teeth out. I heard he
          grabbed Breeny by the collar
          and pushed him.

ShaLann takes a sip of her drink.

                    SHALANN
          Whaaad? No wonder the Airmen
          are terrified of him. Do you
          know that he physically abuses
          the secretary too? He straight
          up fondles her right in front of
          us. It's a frickin' nightmare!

                    PENNY
          She needs to report him.

                    SHALANN
          She's scared she'll lose her
          job or that they'll retaliate
          against her in some other way.
          Either way it's a hard choice.
          Shooting off your mouth can
          have consequences.

BEGIN SERIES OF CHILDHOOD FLASHBACKS

                                        DISSOLVE TO

EXT. FRONT OF CROWLEYS STORE - DAY (FALL 1968)

Five-year-old ShaLann stands between two lovely
women holding shopping bags. The each of the
women is wearing a fur coat, mini dress and go-
go boots. ShaLann is wearing a medium blue pants
suit, white fur jacket and white boots.

Each lady takes ShaLann by the hand as they
stroll toward a soft-top brown Cadillac Coupe.

INT/EXT. PRINCE PETER'S CADILLAC - DAY

Five-year-old ShaLann sits in the front seat of
the Cadillac next to her twenty-seven-year-old
father.

                    PRINCE PETER
          Did your sitters get you some
          nice school clothes?

                    SHALANN
          Yes father.

                    HOOKER #1
          Are we gonna get something to
          eat at the Checkboard before we
          make the drop?

                    HOOKER #2
          No we make the drop first.

                    PRINCE PETER
          Oh, so now you heffas think
          it's okay to talk about my
          business?

ShaLann glances over her left shoulder at one of
the women in the back seat. The woman looks
scared.

                    HOOKER #1
          No Your Highness.

                    HOOKER #2
          Apologies Your Highness.

EXT. CADILLAC IN ALLEY BEHIND MOTWON - DAY
(1968)

Prince Peter sits in his soft top brown
convertible Cadillac in the alley behind the
Motown.

ShaLann sits in the backseat.

                    PRINCE PETER
          Duck down out of sight Lann.

                    SHALANN
          Yes father.

                    SHALANN (V.O) (CONT'D)
          The rich and famous of
          Detroit's music town jonesed
          to do business with my father.

A Black male singer, with a processed doo
hair style, wearing a fancy silver sports
coat enters the alley and reaches into the
passenger side of Prince Peter's Cadillac.

The MUSIC MAN accepts a medium sized brown
paper bag from Prince Peter.

                    MUSIC MAN
          I told my boy Prince Peter is
          always on time.

                    PRINCE PETER
          Don't be spreading my name or
          my business around.

                    MUSIC MAN
          Understood. I'm low key and
          trouble free. We cool?

                    PRINCE PETER
          Cool.

INT. PRINCE PETER'S PENTHOUSE - NIGHT (1968)

Prince Peter and little ShaLann sit on a
cheetah fur sofa watching her UNCLE
RODNEY and UNCLE RODNEY'S FRIEND (BM/with
processed hair) play fight.

Uncle Rodney is holding a white plastic knife
in his closed right hand. The business end of

the plastic knife sticks out of the pinky end
of his fist.

                    UNCLE RODNEY
          I used to be a paratrooper. I can
          kill a guy with almost anything.
          Everything is a weapon. Your
          toothbrush in a guy's eye. Heck
          you can even use your shampoo to
          blind your enemy and create a
          slick spot to trip him up and then
          go to work.

          Right now I'm gonna show you how to
          fight with a knife. See you hold
          the handle in your closed fist so
          that you can punch and or cut and
          stab with the blade like this.

Rodney takes multiple fake swings at his friend.

                    RODNEY'S FRIEND
          Quit playin' man before we
          mess up Pete's stuff.

Little ShaLann giggles.

                    UNCLE RODNEY
          Come on. Come at me.

His friend pulls his handkerchief out of his
pants pocket. He wraps the ends of the
kerchief around each of his hands.

                    RODNEY'S FRIEND
          Alright Cuz, come on then.

Rodney takes another fake swing at his friend.
His friend stretches out his handkerchief and
wraps a corner of the kerchief around each of
his hands.

Rodney fake swings at his friend again, but
this time his friend wraps the kerchief
around Rodney's right wrist.

Rodney uses his left hand to pull another
plastic knife from his waistband and then
puts it against his friend's throat.

                    UNCLE RODNEY
              Got your butt. Always
              have two knives.

Rodney releases his friend.

                    UNCLE
              RODNEY(CONT'D) Slice em in
              the main arteries in the
              neck, inside the wrist or
              the upper inner thigh.
              Here, here and here.

Rodney touches himself in areas to demonstrate
where the main arteries are.

                    UNCLE RODNEY'S FRIEND
              What if the other person has a gun?

                    UNCLE RODNEY
              If I don't have a gun too I'm
              jacked up, but I'll try to talk
              my way out of it.

They are interrupted by a knock at the door.

The friend looks through the peep hole. He
looks at Prince Peter and whispers.

                    UNCLE RODNEY'S FRIEND
              It's that situation.

> PRINCE PETER
> Go to your room and freshen
> up. Don't come out until I
> call you.

> SHALANN (V.O.)
> My father is known for many
> things. The primary one is
> that he is not to be
> messed with.

Little ShaLann goes into the bedroom, but
doesn't completely close the door.

The friend opens the front door.

Little ShaLann crouches down in the bedroom
and peeks through tiny crack between the door
and the frame. Due to furniture blocking part
of her view, she can only see the men in the
living room from their mouth down to their
waist.

Rodney searches the UNIDENTIFIED MAN for
weapons.

> PRINCE PETER
> You violated a major rule by
> coming to my home uninvited.

> UNIDENTIFIED MAN
> I just came here because I
> heard that we have some
> issues. I know I messed up
> with my heroine issue, but I'm
> getting clean and I'm going to
> pay back the money I owe you.
> I'm sorry. I truly apologize.
> I don't want any problems.

                    PRINCE PETER
          Well you have a whole lot
          of problems because you
          can't follow the rules of
          the Kingdom. Let me remind
          you of the rules.

Prince Peter quickly steps behind the man and
wraps his arm around the man's throat.

                    PRINCE PETER (CONT'D)
          Never steal from the Kingdom.
          Don't get high on your own
          supply. Never get high on hair-
          ron cause you jack stuff up. And
          whatever you do...

Peter tightens his grip around the man's
throat.

The man wildly struggles to break free.

                    PRINCE PETER (CONT'D)
          Don't talk about anything
          you see or hear me do. I
          will never, ever forgive
          anybody who puts me or
          family in jeopardy. Not
          anybody!

Peter releases his grip. The man falls to the
floor.

Rodney checks the man's pulse.

                    UNCLE RODNEY
          This negro is dead.

                    PRINCE PETER
          Put him in the kitchen
          until I get Lann out of
          here.

Little ShaLann is visibly shocked. She rushes
to the en-suite bathroom and quietly closes
the door. She flushes the toilet, washes her
hands and starts to brush her teeth.

Prince Peter knocks on the bathroom door.

> PRINCE PETER (CONT'D)
> Come on Lann. It's time to go
> to your Grandma's.

ShaLann opens the bathroom door. She has
toothpaste on her mouth.

> SHALANN
> I'm almost done with my teeth.

END SERIES OF CHILDHOOD FLASHBACKS.

> BACK TO SCENE:

INT. ROCK ISLAND DANCE CLUB - NIGHT

ShaLann stands near a bar sipping her drink.

> PENNY
> He treats y'all worse than
> we're allowed to treat the
> enemy. It's like you're not on
> the same team.

> NESSA
> It's a good thing I'm not
> working there. He'd really have
> a problem with a Black, lesbian,
> witch who's also an
> Environmentalist.

> SHALANN
> What? I didn't know you were a
> tree hugger.

Penny turns to ShaLann.

> PENNY
> Hold up. Hold up. Hold up. Did
> she say Lesbian? Oh Lord you
> done brought me to a gay club.

> SHALANN
> It's not a gay club. It's an
> all people's club.

> PENNY
> That sounds gay to me! I
> rebuke this in the name of
> Jesus! I'm going to the
> restroom and then I'm outta
> here!

Penny storms off to the restroom.

> NESSA
> Ha-ha! Now you owe me a drink.
> See you thought the witch part
> would freak her out. Nope.
> Nothing scares church folks more
> than the gays. Haha-ha!

The bartender hands ShaLann a drink.

> BARTENDER
> The gentleman over there sent
> you a drink.

The bartender points to a group of nerds
sitting at a table.

ShaLann raises her glass and nods thank you to
them.

Nessa waves to two ladies sipping drinks near
the dance floor.

                    NESSA
          Hey look, those two chicks are
          checking us out.

                    SHALANN
          Nah, they're checking you out.
          I'm strictly dickly. You head
          over there and I'll wander over
          here to let that nerd tell me a
          good story. You know. Give him a
          big shot moment for the drink.

                    NESSA
          What you better do is wander your
          butt to the back before your Bama
          roommate discovers that the
          restrooms are unisex.

ShaLann gets flustered and chokes on her
drink.

                    SHALANN
               (coughing)
          Oh shoot! You're right!

ShaLann slams her drink glass down onto the
bar before she rushes towards the restrooms.

Nessa yells to ShaLann.

                    NESSA
          You better hurry! That Bama gone
          come outta that restroom throwing
          tap water and rebuking new wave
          dudes like she's a priest in the
          Exorcist.

Nessa grabs the full drink the nerds sent to
ShaLann.

                    NESSA (CONT'D)
          I guess you won't be needing
          this other cognac will ya?

Nessa sips the drink.

                                   DISSOLVE TO:

INT. POOL TABLE AREA - DAY

ShaLann and Breeny each carry two vases of
flowers towards the exit door.

                    BREENY
          I can't believe they're makin'
          us deliver flowers to Officer's
          wives. I thought it was against
          the regs to make us do personal
          stuff for those guys.

                    SHALANN
          Word! Dang! These flowers are
          missing a card. Go on and I'll
          meet you at the van.

Breeny walks out of the exit.

EXT. SIDE WALK LEADING TO PARKING LOT - DAY

ShaLann is holding a vase filled with flowers
in each arm. As she is walking towards the
squadron's grey delivery van she sees two
male Airman, the squadron's (autistic)
maintenance man and Sergeant Grundle standing
near the van.

Grundle is repeatedly poking his finger into
the chest of the maintenance man as while he
taunts him.

The maintenance man is scared and growing more
upset.

                    SERGEANT GRUNDLE
          Just admit it. All of you
          Mexicans take siestas at
          work. Say it or I'm gonna
          drop kick you.

                    MAINTENANCE MAN
          No. I'm not going to say it
          because it's not true. It's not
          true.

                    SERGEANT GRUNDLE
          Okay I'll give you a five
          second head start. You
          better run fast you mental
          Beaner.

The maintenance man takes off running.

                    SERGEANT GRUNDLE (CONT'D)
          Five mother-fracker!

Sergeant Grundle chases the maintenance man
down and then drop kicks him in his back. The
man falls to the ground, slamming his face on
the asphalt in the parking lot.

Grundle walks over to the two male Airman and
the three of them laugh at the man lying on
the ground.

ShaLann stands at the end of the sidewalk
staring at the aftermath of Grundle's violent
attack in disbelief.

Sergeant Grundle notices ShaLann.

                    SERGEANT GRUNDLE
          Hey Airman Moore. You got a
          problem?

                    SHALANN
          No problem Sergeant.

ShaLann starts walking towards the van.

Sergeant Grundle walks over and block
ShaLann's path.

ShaLann stares forward, trying not to make eye
contact with Sergeant Grundle.

                    SERGEANT GRUNDLE
          You look like you have a
          problem.

ShaLann is worried that Grundle is about to do
something crazy so she squeezes the vases
she's holding tighter.

                    SERGEANT GRUNDLE (CONT'D)
          Get out of my way you frickin'
          Black heffa!

Sergeant Grundle steps forward then slams his
left shoulder hard into ShaLann's left
shoulder.

                    SERGEANT GRUNDLE
          (CONT'D) Careful that you don't
          drop those flowers.

ShaLann steadies herself before getting into
the backseat of the delivery van.

Breeny is sitting in the driver's seat. He
turns around to ShaLann.

                    BREENY
          You okay? That guy is a jack-hole!

ShaLann tosses her head back. She closes her
eyes tightly and trembles as she tries to deal
with the pain in her shoulder.

                    SHALANN
          I'll be okay. Let's get this
          delivery done.

Breeny starts the van then pulls off.

INT. SHALANN'S DORMROOM - NIGHT

The pain in ShaLann's shoulder is more
intense. She stands at the sink in her room.
She pulls off her shirt. She looks at her
shoulder in the mirror. She can see big
bruises on it.

                    SHALANN
          Son-of-a-biscuit! Look at this
          crap!

INT. HEAD OFFICE OF CLUB MANAGEMENT - DAY

ShaLann is so fed up with the abuse from
Grundle that she reports him to the Assistant
Manager at the Head Office.

ShaLann closes the door behind her when she
leaves Assistant Manager's office. She is
hopeful that he will handle the situation.

INT. ASSISTANT MANAGER'S OFFICE - DAY

One by one the Assistant Manager meets with
all of the Airmen and civilians who work with
ShaLann.

ShaLann is the last one to be called into the
Assistant Manager's office.

ShaLann sits in a chair facing the ASSISTANT
MANAGER on the other side of his desk.

                    ASSISTANT MANAGER
          I interviewed everyone. They
          confirmed that Brad is a bit
          of an assertive leader.

                    SHALANN
          Assertive? He literally bruised
          my shoulder.

                    ASSISTANT MANAGER
          Yes, he said that was an
          accident. Sometimes when people
          get dehydrated they bruise
          easily. At any rate, I asked
          Brad to lighten up.

ShaLann stares at him in shock. She loosely
covers her gaping mouth as he continues
talking.

                    ASSISTANT MANAGER (CONT'D)
          As for the more serious matter
          of him sexually harassing
          Rhonda; well she says he makes
          her feel uncomfortable, but she
          refuses to say more than that.
          Others allege that they've seen
          inappropriate behavior, but
          unless she comes forward with
          clear allegations there's
          nothing I can do.

ShaLann looks disappointed as she leaves the
Assistant Manager's office.

INT. RECREATION CENTER - DAY

ShaLann sits alone in her office eating a sandwich while she works on paperwork at her desk.

Sergeant Grundle walks in and closes the door.

> SERGEANT GRUNDLE
> So you tried to get me in trouble with my buddy huh? Well it's really gonna suck for you now. You frickin' sorry Black heffa!

Grundle snatches open the door then storms out.

ShaLann sits at her desk rubbing her forehead with her fingertips. She gets up and leaves her office.

LADIES RESTROOM - DAY

ShaLann is alone in the lady's restroom washing her hands when Rhonda walks in. ShaLann and Rhonda say nothing to each other.

Rhonda goes into a stall to do her business.

The sound of a toilet flushing fills the restroom.

Rhonda comes out of the stall then washes her hands.

Rhonda is about to leave, but pauses at the door.

ShaLann stops what she's doing. She looks at Rhonda's reflection in the mirror.

                    RHONDA
          I'm sorry for not backing you up
          after you came forward to help
          me, but I couldn't because they
          will retaliate against me for
          telling on Brad.

ShaLann turns to look at Rhonda.

                    SHALANN
               (angry)
          Don't you think they're going to
          retaliate against me?

ShaLann starts talking with her hands.

                    SHALANN (CONT'D)
          You know it was a little over
          ten years ago that White women
          were out there using our words
          of equality while you burned
          your bras in protest and
          marched with your fists in the
          air.

ShaLann speaks while pointing her finger at
Rhonda.

                    SHALANN (CONT'D)
          You didn't mean it, but you put
          on a damn good show though.
          See, if you angst filled
          privileged chicks really wanted
          equality, you'd be willing to
          take some lumps just like my
          people did.

ShaLann walks towards the door.

Rhonda speaks through heavy tears.

                    RHONDA
        I'm sorry! I'm really sorry.

ShaLann pauses after she grabs the door
handle. She speaks without turning around.

                    SHALANN
        Ain't that the truth!

ShaLann storms out of the restroom.

EXT. FIELD NEXT TO BASE GYM - DAY

ShaLann is pulling up gasoline soaked weeds
with her bare hands. She stands near a pad
locked green equipment shed. The shed faces
the side of the main base gym.

ShaLann gets a small cut on her right hand
from a weed. Her right hand trembles from the
gasoline stinging her cut.

ShaLann squats down near the shed to untie her
boots.

She braces herself against the shed as she
pulls off her tube socks.

Airman Breeny walks up to ShaLann. He sees a
broken bottle near ShaLann's feet.

                    BREENY
        Watch out for that glass at
        your feet.

                    SHALANN
        Thanks.

                    BREENY
          This is really messed up! I
          can't believe they have you
          out here pulling up gasoline
          soaked weeds.

                    SHALANN
          I'm sure that Grundle and his
          boys in the front office have
          a whole list of crap for the
          number one Airman on their
          crap list. I'll just cover my
          hands with my socks.

ShaLann wraps one of her white tube socks
around each hand. She uses her free hand and
teeth to tie a bunny ears knot on the back of
each hand.

                    BREENY
          Now they'll hammer you for
          being out of uniform. I think I
          know where the key to the shed
          is. I'll find you some gloves.

                    SHALANN
          Cool. Thanks.

Breeny heads through the side door of the gym.

Sergeant Grundle steps out of the side door of
the gym. He stares at ShaLann.

ShaLann squats down to tie her boots.

Sergeant Grundle softly whistles to get
ShaLann's attention. He slides his pointer
finger like a knife across his throat to
threaten ShaLann.

While ShaLann is squatting, she grabs a big
shard of broken glass in each hand. She keeps

her hands behind her back as she stands up. She is steely eyed when she motions with her head for Sgt. Grundle to come at her.

                    SHALANN (CONT'D)
          Come on then!

Grundle pulls a silver lighter out of his right pants pocket.

ShaLann notices the lighter in Grundle's hand. She tenses up to run.

The door to gym flings open. Breeny bursts through the open door; interrupting the scene between ShaLann and Sergeant Grundle.

It starts to rain. Grundle returns the lighter to his pocket and goes back into the gym.

ShaLann drops the shards of glass.

Breeny and ShaLann stand in the rain starring at each other. They breathe hard from the stress of the moment.

INT/EXT. PHONE BOOTH AT GAS STATION - DUSK

ShaLann gets out of her parked car and enters a phone booth.

                    SHALANN (V.O,)
          Once we get out of the hood I
          think that some people think
          that we forget the hood. That's
          mostly true, but what they don't
          know is, that under the wrong
          conditions, it's a real short
          drive back to where we came
          from.

ShaLann drops a quarter in the coin slot of the payphone then dials a number.

          SHALANN (CONT'D)
Hello Father. I have a problem.

ShaLann tells her father about the trouble she is having with Sergeant Grundle.

          SHALANN (V.O.)
I hate to pull this card. Ever since my father's stint in the Army he's been a little twitchy about bigots in the military.

          PRINCE PETER (V.O.)
    (over phone)
Give me all of his information. Check in with me every night. If I don't hear from you there's no place he can hide.

          SHALANN
Yes Father.
                 DISSOLVE TO:

INT. INSPECTOR GENERAL'S OFFICE - DAY

ShaLann sits calmly in a chair while she is being questioned by IG AGENT #1 and IG AGENT #2, two officers at the Inspector General's office.

          SHALANN (V.O.)
I guess someone complained because now I've been summoned to the IG's Office.

                    IG AGENT #1
          Do you feel threatened?

                    SHALANN
          Let me put it this way. Grundle
          has already come for me and
          bruised my shoulder. He also
          threatened to do worse. I promise
          you that any further acts of
          physical harm to me will surely be
          avenged.

                    IG AGENT #2
          Is that a threat?

                    SHALANN
          I believe it's called a conditional
          conclusion.

ShaLann leans forward in her chair.

                    SHALANN (CONT'D)
               (speaks sternly)
          He threatened my life!

                    IG AGENT #2
          Relax. Relax.

ShaLann sees a wedding ring on the hand of Agent
#2.

                    SHALANN
          If your wife told you that her
          boss attacked her and then
          threatened to hurt her further
          wouldn't you want to protect
          her? Maybe avenge her? I have
          people who love me too. They
          will stop at nothing if some
          dude hurts me.

Agent #2 stares at ShaLann and rubs his wedding ring with his thumb while he processes what she just said.

INT. PRIVATE OFFICE AT BASE HQ - AFTERNOON

>   SHALANN (V.O.)
>   By the afternoon Sergeant
>   Grundle is back at his old
>   job at the Head Office.

Sergeant Grundle staples papers at a desk in a private office.

>   DISSOLVE TO:

INT. FAIRBANKS AIRPORT - DUSK

>   SHALANN (V.O.)
>   As for me, I've been
>   shipped to one of the
>   coldest places in America.

ShaLann walks past a sign that reads "Welcome to Fairbanks, Alaska."
>   SHALANN (V.O.)
>   Is this transfer more
>   malice or mercy?

PAUSE PRIMARY FLASHBACK

INT. SHALANN'S BEDROOM - DAY (PRESENT DAY)

ShaLann sits in front of her laptop.

She feels like she's about to throw up.

>   SHALANN
>   Oh God!
ShaLann races to her en-suite toilet and vomits.

After she vomits she opens the medicine cabinet.
The top shelf has rows of colorful nail polish.
The bottom two rows are filled with bottles of
prescription meds.

ShaLann opens a prescription bottle then places
a pill under her tongue.

                    SHALANN (V.O.)
          These Lupus stomach problems
          have gotten so bad that one
          of my five doctors put me on
          a nausea med for cancer
          patients.

ShaLann splashes her face with cold water then
returns to her laptop.

                    SHALANN (V.O.)
          Now, where was I?

                                        BACK TO:

RETURN TO PRIMARY FLASHBACK

INT. FAIRBANKS AIRPORT - DUSK

ShaLann listens to Christmas music while she
waits near the front entrance of the Fairbanks
airport.

ShaLann watches people get hit with blowing
snow as they exit the building.

A MAN and WOMAN LEAVING the AIRPORT walk by
ShaLann wearing snowsuits. They stop at the
entrance to the airport. The couple talk to
each other while they put on their gloves
and hood.

                    MAN AT AIRPORT
          Holy frosted moose balls baby!
          I bet the wind chill is minus
          sixty outside. You know what
          that means?
                    WOMAN AT AIRPORT
          The E.R. you'll go, if you
          write your name in the snow.

The couple laughs as they exit the airport.

ShaLann looks up at a large welcome to Alaska
sign inside of the airport. It has a digital
thermometer that shows the outside temperature
as -50.

ShaLann rolls her eyes when she sees her
crocheted mittens, short winter jacket, jeans
and slouchy leather boots in the reflection of
a window.

She sees a grey military passenger van pull
up.

INT/EXT. VAN ON ALASKA HIGHWAY - DUSK

ShaLann jumps into the front passenger seat of
the van parked on snow blown highway.

She struggles to close the door in the hard
winds, but she manages to slam the passenger
door shut.

                    SHALANN
          Geezus!

ShaLann watches the driver climb in and shut
his door.

MILITARY DRIVER pulls down the hood of his
parka. He looks at ShaLann.

                    MILITARY DRIVER
              Welcome to Alaska!

He looks at ShaLann warming her mitten covered
hands in front of the van's heater vent.

                    MILITARY DRIVER (CONT'D)
              Nice hat and mittens. Don't
              worry, we'll get you Alaska
              geared up today.

                    SHALANN
              What time is it? I think my
              watch is wrong.

                    MILITARY DRIVER
              It's eleven A.M.

                    SHALANN
              It looks like it's almost night
              outside!

                    MILITARY DRIVER
              This is about as much daylight
              as we'll get during the winter,
              but the summers are really
              trippy. I'll never get used to
              seeing daylight at three A.M.

As they make the long drive towards the base,
ShaLann sees several moose standing like
statues a few yards off of the snow blown
highway.

                    SHALANN
              What's up with the moose? Are
              they dead?

The sergeant laughs.

                    MILITARY DRIVER
          Oh the moose-sickles? When the
          temperature drops too low they
          can barely move so they just
          stand still like they're in
          suspended animation.

                    SHALANN
          Whoa! That's freaky.

INT. ENTRANCE TO SHALANN'S OFFICE - DAY

ShaLann meets her new boss in front of a
closed office door.

He hands her a key.

Her boss points to a name plate on the door
with ShaLann Moore's name on it.

INT. SHALANN'S PRIVATE OFFICE - DAY

ShaLann sits at her desk adding numbers on a
large calculator.

                    SHALANN (V.O.)
          I could complain to any and
          every one about how I got a
          raw deal and was shipped to
          the land of moose-sickles
          or I can suck it up and
          make the best of it.

                              DISSOLVE TO:

EXT. BEACH AT BIRCH LAKE - DAY

                    SHALANN (V.O.)
          I choose the latter.

ShaLann speeds by the front of the Lake Lodge
on a four wheeler. She drags a wood pallet
behind her to smooth out the sand on the
lakeshore.

                    SHALANN (V.O.)
               It's a good thing too. The
               squadron overlords have been
               so impressed with my sunny
               demeanor, that they assigned
               me to run the Lodge at the
               lake.

ShaLann zooms past the Lake Lodge on her four
wheeler again.

                    SHALANN
               It looks like this is a mercy
               assignment after all. Woo!
               Hoo!

INT. LODGE RESERVATION DESK AND SNACK BAR - DAY

ShaLann assists a female guest from behind the
reservations counter. She hands the woman a
small brown paper bag filled with food and a
key.
                    SHALANN
               You're in cabin number eight.

EXT. COPPER RIVER HORSE RIDING TRAIL - DAY

                    SHALANN (V.O.)
               I'm finally back on track
               providing R and R to my
               mission tired brothers and
               sisters in arms.

A guide wearing a cowboy hat leads ShaLann and
a group of Airman on horseback down a hill to
the Copper River. The group admires tree lined
mountain cliffs along the trail.

In the distance they can see two large white
water rafts and four guides sitting on the
riverbank.

EXT. COPPER RIVER - DAY

White water rafting on the Copper River.

ShaLann and a group of Airman scream with glee
when their raft goes up and down peaks in the
river.

EXT. ALASKAN CAMP GROUNDS - DAY

ShaLann and the group of Airman sit on a
mixture of lawn chairs, big logs and boulders
while they enjoy a bbq rib dinner around a
campfire.

A male guide in a cowboy sits down next to
ShaLann. He grabs a guitar and starts singing
to the group.

                              DISSOLVE TO:

INT. THE ENLISTED CLUB - NIGHT (1990)

                    SHALANN (V.O.)
          By snowfall I'm working at the
          Enlisted Club. I gotta tell
          ya, dim lights and boozed up
          Airmen give Club Managers a
          peek behind the veil that most
          will never see.

BEGIN MONTAGE OF SCENES AT ENLISTED CLUB

People are drinking, dancing and enjoying
themselves at the crowded Enlisted Club.

ShaLann watches a married guy flirt with a
young woman at the end of the bar. ShaLann can
see tan lines on the finger where his wedding
ring should be.

ShaLann sees two drunk young men allow the
back of their hands and fingers to slowly rub
together when they think no one is watching as
they leave the club.

ShaLann notices that there are groups of young
Black females sitting without male company.

ShaLann also notices that Black males are
dancing with and leaving the Club with Asian,
White or Latino women.

END MONTAGE.

                    BARTENDER #2
          These Black Airmen are like
          kids in an ice cream shop
          that sample every flavor
          except chocolate.

                    SHALANN
          Interesting.

                              DISSOLVE TO:

EXT. LIGHTED CROSS COUNTRY SKI TRAIL - DUSK

                    SHALANN (V.O.)
          Oh well.

DAVID, a cute White guy with dark wavy hair,
in his late twenties teaches ShaLann how to
cross country ski.

ShaLann stumbles and falls.

The guy helps her up.

                    DAVID
          I got you snow bunny.

                                        DISSOLVE TO:

EXT. NEAR LOG CABIN - NIGHT

ShaLann and David dance near a snow covered
cabin under the Northern Lights. David sings
a Hard Habit to Break in ShaLann's ear as
they dance.

                                        DISSOLVE TO:

EXT. ALASKA HOT SPRINGS GROTO - NIGHT

ShaLann sits nude in a Hot Spring with her
arms resting on the stones beside her. The
curves of her breasts glow under the camp
lights.

                    SHALANN (V.O.)
          When working in an ice cream
          shop where Black guys no
          longer eat chocolate...

David stands bare chested in steamy water
several feet in front of ShaLann. The warm
water barely covers his hips. Camp lights
highlight David's chiseled physique.

                    SHALANN (V.O.)
          Fraternize with a cute,
          White Captain named David
          who does.

David wades towards ShaLann. He dives beneath
the water then rises with his head between
ShaLann's knees. She closes her eyes and
tosses her head back while she enjoys his
passion.

DISSOLVE TO:

EXT. FRONT OF COMMISSARY - DAY

ShaLann is carrying a shopping bag when she
exits the Commissary.

ShaLann rushes over to help a very pregnant
MRS. SHOO after she sees one of her grocery
bags break - spilling canned goods onto the
snow covered ground.

                  SHALANN
        Let me get those for you
        Mrs. Shoo.
                  MRS. SHOO
        Oh thank you.
ShaLann removes the spices from her bag and
shoves them into the pockets of her uniform.
ShaLann bends down and picks up the cans then
them into the empty bag. She puts the bag into
the back of Mrs. Shoo's SUV and then helps her
load the rest of her groceries into the truck.

                  SHALANN
        I haven't seen you at the
        Computer Lab in a couple of
        months.
                  MRS. SHOO
        Yeah. After my husband
        deployed, I figured it would
        be easier if I put my career
        on hold to take care of two
        kids and manage this little
        guy when he makes his debut.

                  SHALANN
        Oh. That's too bad. You're
        the third officer's wife who
        told me she quit her job
        this week.

                    MRS. SHOO
          Don't be sad. I knew the
          sacrifices I'd have to make
          when I married a pilot. We do
          what we have to do to serve
          the country.

                    SHALANN
          Yes, ma'am. You have a great day.

                              DISSOLVE TO:

INT. MOTEL ROOM - NIGHT

ShaLann and David lay in a wood paneled motel
room cuddling.

                    DAVID
          I was thinking that we get
          along great. Why don't we
          get married? You can get out
          and then we could make us
          some cute babies.

ShaLann sits up.

                    SHALANN
               (surprised)
          Marriage, no Air Force
          career and babies? That's
          a lot to digest.

                    DAVID
          You can pursue a college
          degree before we have kids
          of course.

                    SHALANN
          Oh of course.

                    DAVID
          See I covered all of the
          bases. All you have to do
          is say yes.

                  SHALANN
          Those are big moves. I'll
          need to think about it.

EXT. PARKING LOT OF MOTEL - NIGHT

ShaLann backs her car out of a parking space.

David leans against the passenger side of his
vehicle with his head resting against his
crossed arms.

                 SHALANN (V.O.)
          I told David no. There's no
          way that I'm going to end up
          unemployed, raising a bunch of
          kids with no man around. Hell
          I could've had that bullcrap
          in Detroit. Except in this
          case I'd get a spectacular
          wedding ring. I'll pass on the
          illusion.

                              DISSOLVE TO:

EXT. LODGE AT BIRCH LAKE - DAY

ShaLann stands at the top of steps of the Lodge
watching laughing children play near the swings
in front of the lake.

A couple in a paddle boat point at a moose
sipping water on the other side of the lake.

                    SHALANN (V.O.)
          Everything is back to about
          as picture perfect as it can
          get. I wish I could stay in
          this happy moment forever.

EXT. MULTIPLE ROCKET LAUNCHER - NIGHT

Three fire blazing missiles consecutively launch
from an Army Multiple Launch Rocket System.

INT. MESS HALL IN ALASKA - DAY (AUG 1990)
Several Airmen stand in front of a television
in the Chow Hall watching a NEWSCASTER.

                    NEWSCASTER (V.O.)
          Breaking news: Saddam Hussein
          just invaded the country of
          Kuwait. He also launched scud
          missiles into Israel.

A news clip of Saddam Hussein waving from a
tank appears on the TV.

                    SHALANN (V.O.)
          Unfortunately, the butt-head
          in charge of Iraq decided to
          disrupt world peace.

A news clip of President H. Bush addressing
the nation appears on the TV.

                    SHALANN (V.O.)
          In response to the invasion of
          Kuwait and threats to the
          world's oil supply, President
          George H. Bush orders the
          commencement of Operations
          Desert Shield and Desert
          Storm. Time for us warfighters
          in blue to do what we do.

INT. GRAPHIC DESIGN ROOM - NIGHT (AUG 1990)

                    SHALANN (V.O.)
          Just like thousands of Airmen
          who've gone before us, it's
          time for us to do what we
          were trained to do.

The Valley Girl Airman who is now a Staff
Sergeant uses a large cutting machine to cut
wall sized maps of the Middle East.

She stuffs a rolled up wall map into a long
cardboard tube.

INT. FLIGHTCREW WAR ROOM - DAY

A Colonel stands in front of a large wall map
of the Middle East holding a wood pointer. He
briefs a group of flight crew members.

EXT. MONTAGE AIR FORCE JETS AND PLANES FLY TO

WAR - DAY Air Force flight crews race to their

fighter jets.

Air Force crews load missiles onto fighter jets.

One by one fighter jets take to the skies.

END MONTAGE.

EXT. IRAQ DESERT - DAY

Air Force fighter jets fire several missiles at
a line of Iraqi tanks.

Big explosions occur when Iraqi tanks are
destroyed by fighter jet missiles.

EXT. B-52 BOMBER AREA ON FLIGHT LINE - NIGHT

A large PSYOPS bomber plane sits on the flight
line.

The PSYOPS air crew wheels a fifteen-thousand-
pound bomb towards the B-52 Bomber.

The side of explosive has the words shake,
rattle and run painted in the middle of a
picture of a giant penis.

EXT. STREETS OF IRAQI VILLAGE - DAY

Iraqi villagers pick up American propaganda
leaflets with Arabic words and Saddam Hussein's
picture on them.

The leaflets blame the war on Saddam Hussein.

INT. MAKESHIFT FIELD MORGUE IN IRAQ - DAY

                    SHALANN (V.O.)
          And just like thousands of
          others who've gone before
          us, the ultimate price is
          paid.

Staff Sergeant Breeny zips up a body bag
containing the body of Staff Sergeant Campbell.

INT. REAR HULL OF AIR CARRIER PLANE - DAY

Air Force Officers dressed in blue uniforms sit
quietly while strapped in along the rear wall
of plane.

                    SHALANN (V.O.)
          With all that we do, the
          hardest part is when we
          transport our most
          valuable cargo.

Two Officers look emotionless at rows of
American flag draped coffins displayed in the
cargo hold.

EXT. ALASKA BASE HEADQUARTERS BUILDING - DAY

A flag flies at half-staff in front of the
headquarters building on Eielson AFB, Alaska.

> SHALANN (V.O.)
> I just got orders to Germany.
> You know what that means?

INT. ALASKA BASE IMMUNIZATION CLINIC - DAY

> SHALANN (V.O.)
> More frickin' shots.

An Immunizations Technician prepares a needle.

ShaLann shuts her eyes and grimaces as she
takes a series of injections in her arm.

The Shot Tech gives ShaLann a little packet of
Motrin.

ShaLann looks at the packet in the palm of
hand and then gives the Shot Technician the
side eye.

EXT. WEAPONS RANGE - DAY
> SHALANN (V.O.)
> It also means more warfighter
> training.

ShaLann stands firing at a paper target with an
M16 semiautomatic rifle.

ShaLann stands while firing a semiautomatic
handgun at a paper target.

A trainer hands ShaLann her paper target.

ShaLann holds a bullet riddled paper target in her hands. The target has a note on it that says, "Two shots away from marksman."

INT. WEAPONS SAFETY CLASSROOM - DAY

ShaLann stands in a firearms safety classroom cleaning a disassembled semiautomatic rifle (M-16).

ShaLann completes the assembly of her weapon and lays it on the table.

> SHALANN (V.O.)
> But before I head overseas I
> get sent home on leave.

> DISSOLVE TO:

INT. RANCE'S APARTMENT - DAY

A handsome thirty-year-old Black man named RANCE stands in the doorway of his apartment.

> RANCE
> Heeey! Come on in.

Rance shuts his door when ShaLann enters his apartment.

Rance swoops ShaLann up in his arms and kisses her on the lips. He squeezes her bottom.

ShaLann gently pushes him away.

> SHALANN
> Hold up. Doesn't your greedy
> butt have a girlfriend?

                    RANCE
          There's nothing wrong with a
          little hello bottom squeeze for
          old times sake.

Rance steps back and looks ShaLann up and down.

                    RANCE (CONT'D)
          Look at you big timer;
          looking like a noonday
          snack.

                    SHALANN
          Nawl you're the big timer. I
          heard you're working with the
          Purple One.

                    RANCE
          I'm doing a few thangs.

                    SHALANN
          A few thangs? I saw your
          performance on Soul Train big
          timer. Great job!

                    RANCE
          Thank ya kindly.

                    SHALANN
          Hey I'm about to head up to
          the Beauty Shop to see our
          buddy. My GPS is trippin'.
          Can you give me directions?

                    RANCE
          I have to head up that
          way to pick up my girl.
          Follow me.

EXT. BEAUTY SHOP'S PARKING LOT - DAY

                    RANCE
               (to ShaLann)
          When we get in here don't say
          anything about being at my
          house or me kissing you.

                    SHALANN
          Why would I do that anyway?

                    RANCE
          I'm just sayin'.

INT. NAT'S BEAUTY SHOP - DAY
ShaLann and Rance enter the Beauty Shop.

NAT is curling a woman's hair BEAUTY CUSTOMER
#1 while she eats potato chips.

                    RANCE
          Hey! Look who I just ran into.

                    NAT
          Welcome home lady.
          Everybody this is my Ex
          ShaLann from eons ago.
          ShaLann everybody.

                    SHALANN
          Heeey Everybody!

                    NAT

          ShaLann's in the Air Force.
          She lives in Alaska.

                    BEAUTY CUSTOMER #1
          Do you fly planes?

                    SHALANN
          No.

                    BEAUTY CUSTOMER #2
                      (bad English)
            Oooo, do you live in a igloo?

                      SHALANN
            No I live in an apartment.

                       RANCE
            Come over here ShaLann. I
            want to introduce you to my
            Girl.

Rance is standing in front of a blond haired
Black woman. His body is blocking her face.

                    RANCE (CONT'D)
            ShaLann this is...

Rance steps aside. It's SHERELLE.

                    SHALANN (V.O.)
            Oh my goodness it's the famous
            pop star Sherelle.

                      SHALANN
                    (to Sherelle)
            Pleased to meet you.

                      SHERELLE
            Nice to meet you too.
            Thank you for your
            service.

ShaLann glances at Rance.

                    SHALANN (V.O.)
            This negro looks like he's
            begging me not to ruin his
            situation.

Nat notices that his buddy Rance is in trouble.

                    NAT
                (to ShaLann)
        You hanging out tonight?

                  SHALANN
        My sister is taking me to
        some U.B. Club.

                    NAT
        That's in a rough part of town.

                CUSTOMER #1
        Don't be dissin' the U.B.
        That club is kinda upscale.

Customer #1 picks her front teeth with the
baby fingernail on her right hand.

                SHALANN (V.O.)
        Kinda upscale club in a bad
        neighborhood is code for
        Gangster Bougie.

INT. U.B. CLUB - NIGHT

ShaLann, Ang and Lena walk into the U.B. Club
looking fly.

Gangster dudes are in the club wearing real
fur coats and big gold chains.

Chicks wearing classy club outfits use a straw
to sip from small bottles of champagne.

Dudes eat chicken wings with their thumb and
first two fingers to avoid getting their pinky
ring dirty.

ShaLann sees an ex-boyfriend RICKY sitting with
a group of people in the VIP section.

He's wearing a tan mink coat. He's sitting next to a beautiful woman (RICKY'S GIRLFRIEND).

ShaLann walks over to his table.

> SHALANN
> (smiling)
> Hey Rickie, how you doin'?

Ricky stands up and gives ShaLann a hug.

> RICKY
> Hey lady! Long time no see. You on vacation from the Air Force?

> SHALANN
> Yes.

> RICKY'S GIRLFRIEND
> Where are you stationed at?

> SHALANN
> Alaska, but I'm heading out to Germany tomorrow.

> RICKY'S GIRLFRIEND
> Wow that's nice!

> SHALANN
> (to Ricky's girlfriend)
> Mind if I borrow Ricky for a dance.

> RICKY'S GIRLFRIEND
> Go right ahead.

ShaLann and Ricky do an old school two-step. The DJ puts on a 90s slow jam. ShaLann and Ricky slow dance.

> RICKY
> This slow dancing gone get me in trouble.

                    SHALANN
          Nawl. Your girl seems like an
          honorable woman. You'll be
          fine.

                    RICKY
          I'm surprised to see you in
          here. I thought you hated the
          Game.

                    SHALANN
          I do. This was my sister's
          idea. I'm not surprised to
          see you in here Maserati
          Rick.

                    RICKY
          Oh! You heard about that huh?

                    SHALANN
          I still read the trades. Well
          let me send you back to your
          girl. I'm gonna get a drink and
          bounce.

Ricky returns to his seat.

ShaLann nods thank you to Ricky's girlfriend.

ShaLann heads to the bar.

Suddenly a woman screams.

                    SOME DUDE
          They shooting outside.

ShaLann directs LENA and ANG (short for
Angela) to get under a table near a wall.

                         SHALANN
                   (to Lena and Ann)
                 Stay low and against the
                 wall to avoid a stampede.

Finally, everything calms down.

ShaLann, Lena and Ann leave the club.

EXT. U.B. CLUB'S PARKING LOT - NIGHT

ShaLann opens the driver's door to her grey
rental car.

Ann and Lena stand on the passenger side of
the car.
                         LENA
                 ShaLann come look at this.

ShaLann heads to the passenger side of the
car.

ShaLann, Lena and Ann stare at the passenger
side of the car.

The passenger side is riddled with bullet
holes.

                         SHALANN
                   (angry)
                 Look at this damage!

                         LENA
                 Welcome back to Detroit.

                         SHALANN
                 This place is a warzone!
                 We could've been killed!

                    ANN
          Don't relax. Those people at the
          rental car place probably gone
          kill you when they see this
          damage.

                    LENA
          Yup.

ShaLann looks to her left then side eyes Lena
and Ann.

                              DISSOLVE TO:

EXT. ENTRY GATE RHEIN MAIN AFB GERMANY - DAY

An Air Force police officer checks ID cards
before waving cars through the main entrance
of Rhein Main Air Force Base, Germany.

INT. OFFICE - DAY

ShaLann, now Staff Sergeant Moore is wearing
her Battle Dress Uniform while sitting in a
private office talking on the phone.

Three posters of people enjoying recreation
activities in Germany, France and England hang
on the wall behind her.

                    SHALANN (V.O.)
          Thankfully I survived all of
          that Detroit drama. I'm now
          enjoying my new job as Program
          Manager of the Recreation
          Center.

ShaLann hangs up the phone. She grabs a stack
of index cards and her hat then stands up to
leave her office.

INT. FIRST SERGEANT'S OFFICE IN GERMANY - DAY

The First Sergeant is sitting at his desk.
The walls of his office are decorated with
German and motivational posters.

ShaLann appears in his open doorway wearing a
jogging suit. She's holding index cards in her
hand.

> SHALANN
> (smiling)
> Guten tag First Sergeant.

> FIRST SERGEANT
> Guten tag. Is that the
> General's opening remarks
> for the USO show?

> SHALANN
> Yes, it is.

ShaLann hands him the index cards.

> SHALANN (CONT'D)
> I thought I'd drop it off
> before I go for a run.

> FIRST SERGEANT
> You better add speech writing
> as bullet on your resume when
> you retire.

> SHALANN
> I only write the opening
> remarks. Anyway, I'm gonna hit
> the track now. Have a great
> weekend First Sergeant.

> FIRST SERGEANT
> Hold up on that run Moore.

He hands ShaLann a big yellow envelope with
small holes in it.

                    SHALANN
          Um, isn't it bad luck to
          give someone a Holey-Joe
          on a Friday afternoon?

                    FIRST SERGEANT
          You got orders to deploy to
          Turkey on a four-month
          humanitarian mission. I need
          for you to start out-
          processing right away.

ShaLann straightens up and takes a serious
posture.

                    SHALANN
          Right away Shirt.

INT. IMMUNIZATION CLINIC IN GERMANY - DAY

ShaLann sits in the Shot Clinic with her over
shirt off. She rolls up the left sleeve of her
t-shirt to take more shots. IMMUNIZATION TECHS
#1 and #2 stand in the room preparing needles.

                    SHALANN
          I just had a bunch of shots
          in Alaska so what am I
          getting today.

                    IMMUNIZATION TECH #1
          Flu plus g.g. in oral and
          injection form. Here's the Flu
          shot.

The Shot Tech injects ShaLann with a Flu shot.

                    SHALANN
          I just had a g.g. shot a few
          months ago. Look at my shot
          record.

ShaLann holds up her shot record and points to
the area where her immunizations are listed.
She notices that there are dates stamped and a
Tech's name listed, but no drug name in a few
spaces. She also notices that the g.g. shot
isn't listed.

The Shot Tech looks at the record.

>   IMMUNIZATION TECH #2
>   Looks like you need the g.g.
>   shot. Here, take this pill.

ShaLann swallows the small white pill and
rinses it down with water in a white paper
cup.

>   SHALANN
>   Isn't that strange that I
>   have date stamps in my shot
>   record, but no drugs listed?

The Shot Techs shrug their shoulders.

Worried about the issues in her shot record,
ShaLann looks at the two Shot Techs with
suspicion.

>   IMMUNIZATION TECH #1
>   I don't know anything about
>   that. This g.g. shot might
>   hurt so think happy thoughts.

Tech interrupts her.

>   IMMUNIZATION TECH #1
>   You take this shot in your arm.

>   SHALANN
>   That's odd. I thought that
>   it went in your hip.

                    IMMUNIZATION TECH #2
          Nah, this way it really boosts
          your immune system. It'll make
          you a super soldier.

ShaLann holds up her right hand for the Shot
Techs to pause.

                    SHALANN
          Hold up. Wait a min...

The Shot Tech quickly injects ShaLann with the
needle.

ShaLann grimaces from the sudden injection.

                    SHALANN (CONT'D)
          Dammit!

                    IMMUNIZATION TECH #1
          Move your arm around so the
          medicine will hurt less when it
          hits your system.

                    SHALANN
          Wha...?

ShaLann's words are cut off when she gets hit
with a long burning pain in her left arm.

                    SHALANN (CONT'D)
          Son of a buster that hurt! I've
          never experienced delayed pain
          like that after a shot. Are you
          sure that was a g.g. shot?

                    IMMUNIZATION TECH #2
          Yes.

                    IMMUNIZATION TECH #1
          Don't forget to take Motrin for
          the pain and fever.

ShaLann walks out of the room.

INT. IN-PROCESSING INCIRLIK AIR BASE - DAY

SUPER OVER BLACK: "Tent City, Incirlik, Turkey"

A male TURKISH DRIVER meets ShaLann at the in-processing building.

>   TURKISH DRIVER
>   You Moore?

>   SHALANN
>   Yes.

>   TURKISH DRIVER
>   You early. I take you to
>   Commander.

The driver picks up ShaLann's suitcase and a long green duffel bag.

>   SHALANN
>   I think that I should wait for
>   my sponsor Staff Sergeant
>   Leticia Parker.

>   TURKISH DRIVER
>   She's outside. Smoke break.

EXT. IN-PROCESSING BUILDING - DAY

ShaLann and the driver exit the building and walk towards Staff Sergeant LETICIA PARKER.

Sergeant Parker sees her driver walking with ShaLann. She quickly puts out her cigarette in a butt can.

>   TURKISH DRIVER
>   Moore is here.

                    SHALANN
          Hey Leticia. Nice to put a
          face with a name.

                    LETICIA PARKER
          I thought that you wouldn't be
          here for another half hour.
          Let's get you over to meet the
          Commander and the Mayor of
          Tent City.

                    SHALANN
          The Mayor?

                    LETICIA PARKER
          He's a Major, but we call him
          The Mayor.

Leticia notices the driver struggling to lift
one of ShaLann's bags.

                    LETICIA PARKER (CONT'D)
          Girl you brought a lot of bags.

                    SHALANN
          Some of our guys said that
          they hung out during down
          time, so I brought my work,
          church AND party clothes.

                    LETICIA PARKER
          Don't let The Chief hear you
          say that. She's a little
          annoyed that some people think
          this is a cushy deployment.

EXT. GRAVEL ROAD NEAR COMMANDER'S OFFICE - DAY

ShaLann gets out of the van. She notices Army
troops jogging in formation on base.

Leticia points to different areas of the base as she speaks.

                    LETICIA PARKER
          Down that road is the Commissary.
          Over there is the ladies shower
          hut. Always wear your shower
          shoes in there or you'll get toe
          leprosy or some crap.

                    SHALANN
          Copy that!

                    LETICIA PARKER
          Oh and if a siren goes off
          while you're in the shower get
          out immediately. There may be
          toxins in the water.

                    SHALANN
          Yikes! Copy that.

                    LETICIA PARKER
          Our tent is only three tents
          away from the shower hut.

                    SHALANN
          That's cool. I can use a
          shower, some Motrin for this
          nagging headache and a nap.

The driver unloads ShaLann's bags and sits them on the gravel road. He begins to get back in the vehicle.

                    LETICIA PARKER
          Driver wait. Please take the
          bags to the ladies' tent area.

The driver waves his hands and shakes his head no.

                    LETICIA PARKER (CONT'D)
          I'll pay you.

                    TURKISH DRIVER
          No allowed in ladies' area.

                    LETICIA PARKER
          Oh come on man!

                    TURKISH DRIVER
          No. I lose job. No allowed!

The driver yells something in Arabic and gets
in the van. He spins up gravel towards Parker
and ShaLann as he drives off.

ShaLann brushes dust off of her uniform.

                    SHALANN
          Well damn!

THE CHIEF watches the two Sergeants from the
doorway of a small building marked Commander's
Headquarters.

                    THE CHIEF
          Hey Parker. Is that Sergeant
          Moore?

                    LETICIA PARKER
          Yes ma'am.

                    THE CHIEF
          Bring her bags inside while we
          wait on the Commander. You don't
          want a spider to crawl into her
          gear.

                    LETICIA PARKER
          Yes Chief.

INT. WAITING AREA NEAR COMMANDER'S OFFICE - DAY

The Chief walks out of her office to greet
ShaLann.

                    THE CHIEF
          Welcome to Turkey. It looks
          like you were issued a lot of
          gear. What's all of those
          pointy things sticking up in
          your duffel bag?

Leticia steps back out of the sight of The
Chief. Parker mouths no to Moore. She puts her
finger over her lip indicating for ShaLann to
keep quiet.

The Chief cracks a devious smile when she sees
Parker's antics in the reflection of a picture
hanging on the wall behind ShaLann.

                    SHALANN
          It's just my gear civilian
          clothes Chief.

                    THE CHIEF
          Open it up so that I can see
          what kind of gear they issued
          you.

ShaLann opens her duffel bag and pulls out a
pair of sneakers and sweats.

                    THE CHIEF (CONT'D)
          Uh-huh keep going.

ShaLann pulls out three pairs of high heeled
shoes, two pairs of sandals and two pairs of
low heeled pumps.

                    THE CHIEF (CONT'D)
          What's all those shoes for?

                    SHALANN
          Church and special occasions.

                   THE CHIEF
          Riiigghht. Keep goin'.

ShaLann pulls out a black cloth bag about the
size of two hat boxes.

The Chief nods at the bag as indication for
ShaLann to open it and pull out the items in
it.

ShaLann pulls out two sweat shirts with writing
on them:
Where Da Party At and Party Princess. She also
pulls out a Santa hat, small neon flash lights,
noise makers and gold and purple beaded
necklaces.

                   THE CHIEF (CONT'D)
          I thought Parker's bags were
          bad, but Moore you got the
          Disco Queen over here beat.
          Put your stuff away before the
          Commander returns.

ShaLann quickly returns her things to her
duffel bag.

                   THE CHIEF (CONT'D)
          The problem with most of the
          people who deploy here is that
          they've gotten soft from riding
          the desk. Well it's my job to get
          you right and tight. Disco Queen
          Parker is already on twelve hour
          shifts. Party Princess Moore your
          shift starts at midnight tonight
          at the Morale Tent.

                    SHALANN
                (upset)
        But Chief that's in six hours!
        My orders say that I'm not
        supposed to start work until
        tomorrow.

                    THE CHIEF
        It will be tomorrow at 12:01 am.

                    SHALANN
        Chief!

                    THE CHIEF
        Hey, at least you have a
        few hours to take a nap.
        Some of these guys have to
        go to work straight off the
        plane. I'm being nice.

                    SHALANN
                (emotionless)
        Yes Chief.

INT. MORALE TENT - NIGHT

ShaLann goes to work in a huge tent. The tent
houses a snack bar that sits between a movie
theater and twelve old wooden phone booths.

                    SHALANN (V.O.)
        And so the monotony of
        working twelve hour shifts
        begins.

ShaLann stands behind the counter of the Snack
Bar.

                    SHALANN (V.O.)
        Sell food to the troops.

ShaLann hands a bag of chips to a guy.

                    SHALANN (V.O.)
          List the daily movies.

ShaLann writes three movie titles and their
descriptions on a white board across from the
snack bar.

                    SHALANN (V.O.)
          Clean the phone booths.

ShaLann wipes the glass of a wooden phone
booth with Windex and paper towels.

EXT. DUMPSTER BEHIND MORALE TENT - DAY

                    SHALANN (V.O.)
          Take out the trash.

ShaLann tosses a big bag of trash into a
dumpster behind the tent.

INT. SHALANN'S COT IN TENT - DAY

                    SHALANN (V.O.)
          Get some frickin' sleep and repeat.

An exhausted ShaLann falls on her back onto her
cot. She wraps herself in an olive green
blanket.

BEGIN MONTAGE OF SCENES AT MORALE TENT AND
DUMPSTER

INT. MORALE TENT - NIGHT

ShaLann slaps a bag of chips in a guy's hand.

ShaLann writes the word MOVIES on a white board.

ShaLann Windexes and wipes the glass in wooden
phone booth.

EXT. DUMPSTER BEHIND TENT - DAY

                    SHALANN (V.O.)
          Take out the trash. Repeat.

ShaLann tosses a big trash bag into a dumpster.

                    SHALANN (V.O.)
          Repeat.

INT. MORALE TENT - NIGHT

ShaLann slaps a bag of chips in a guy's hand.

ShaLann writes the word MOVIES on a white board.

ShaLann Windexes and wipes the glass in wooden
booth.

EXT. DUMPSTER BEHIND TENT - DAY

                    SHALANN (V.O.)
          Take out the trash.

ShaLann tosses a big bag of trash into dumpster.

                    SHALANN (V.O.)
          Repeat.

EXT. DUMPSTER BEHIND TENT - DAY

                    SHALANN (V.O.)
          Take out the trash.

ShaLann tosses a big bag of trash into dumpster.

                    SHALANN (V.O.)
        Repeat.

EXT. DUMPSTER BEHIND TENT - DAY

                    SHALANN (V.O.)
         Take out the fricking trash.

ShaLann tosses a big bag of trash into dumpster.

END MONTAGE.

EXT. DUMPSTER BEHIND MORALE TENT - DAY

ShaLann is walking away from the garbage
dumpster towards the rear entrance of the
Morale Tent when she is waved down by The
Chief.

The Chief walks quickly towards ShaLann.

                    THE CHIEF
              (sweetly sings name)
         Heeeey Moore!

ShaLann is exhausted after her twelve-hour
shift. She slowly turns towards the Chief.

                    SHALANN
         Yes Chief.

The Chief appears happier and more polite than
usual.

                    THE CHIEF
         How you doin girlfriend?

ShaLann looks at the Chief with suspicion.

                    SHALANN
         Tired, but - fine.

                    THE CHIEF
          How would you like to do me
          a favor?

ShaLann purses her lips and side eyes The Chief.

                    SHALANN
          Like pick up a pizza and
          cigarettes favor or help you
          hide a body kind of favor?

The Chief laughs and wraps her arm around
ShaLann's shoulder.

ShaLann side eyes the Chief's hand on her
shoulder.
                    THE CHIEF
          Girl you crazy! Since you
          have experience writing
          speeches for Generals and
          arranging events for
          Officers, I thought I'd ask
          if you wouldn't mind
          replacing me on a two-day
          humanitarian trip to Iraq.

ShaLann jerks away from the Chief.

                    SHALANN
          Iraq? This is definitely a
          help you hide the body kind
          of favor!
                    THE CHIEF
          You'll fly into the safe zone
          the day before Turkey Day.
          Oversee the setup for the
          dignitaries. Make sure
          everything looks and tastes
          like Thanksgiving. Take some
          of those drawings the school
          kids sent to us.

                    THE CHIEF (CONT'D)
          Maybe cook those Sweet Potato
          Pies you brought to the
          potluck. Bing, bam, boom
          you're out of there the next
          morning. See. Too easy!

                    SHALANN
          I don't know Chief.

                    THE CHIEF
          I'll owe you big time.

ShaLann folds her arms and stares at the Chief
for a few seconds.

                    SHALANN
          Really? Like what?

                    THE CHIEF
          How about one hour off, every
          three days for one month.

ShaLann laughs.

                    SHALANN
          You gotta do much better than
          that. That dead body you're
          trying to hide is starting to
          stank.

                    THE CHIEF
          Okay. Okay. Three hours off,
          every three days until you go
          back to Germany.

                    SHALANN
          Deal.

The Chief gives ShaLann an enthusiastic hug.

                    THE CHIEF (CONT'D)
          Great and um, let's keep this
          between us. We don't want the
          Commander thinking I'm hooking
          you up on the schedule.

As the Chief walks away she yells to ShaLann.

                    THE CHIEF (CONT'D)
          Take a parka because it's cold
          on the copter. Stay out of the
          Red Zone and don't screw this up.
                    SHALANN
          Copter? As in helicopter?

ShaLann rolls her eyes as she watches the Chief
walk down the gravel road.

                    SHALANN (V.O.)
          Like I'm going to say no and
          incur the wrath of a Chief.
          Besides, this high ranking
          heffa just got out of a
          holiday humanitarian mission
          that she doesn't want the
          Commander to know about. It's
          like an unlimited load of get
          out of Hell free cards just
          rained down on my head.

INT/EXT. PASSENGER CABIN ARMY HELICOPTER - DAY

Two Army helicopters sit idling on a flight
line.

An Army Warrant Officer named CHAD sits in the
passenger cabin of one of the helicopters. He
watches a parka wearing ShaLann carry a big
green duffel bag to the helicopter he's sitting
in.

Chad helps ShaLann get into the helicopter.

                    CHAD
          Welcome aboard.

Chad straps ShaLann into the seat across from
him and gives her a set of bulky headphones.

Other Warrant Officers also board the copter.
The last one in closes the door.

The sound of the rotors of the copter grow
louder as they spin faster.

Chad sees that ShaLann looks visibly tense and
afraid.

                    CHAD (CONT'D)
          First time on a helicopter?

ShaLann shakes her head up and down yes.

                    CHAD (CONT'D)
          I've done this hundreds of times.
          Keep your eyes on me. You don't
          get afraid until I get afraid
          okay?

                    SHALANN
          Okay.

ShaLann smiles and relaxes her posture.

One after the other, the Army helicopters take
flight.

EXT. HOUSE COMPOUND - DAY

Wind from the rotors of the helicopter ShaLann
is riding in blows a dust cloud around a lonely
two story home in the desert of Northern Iraq.

Sandbags and barbed wire surround the Compound.

The other helicopter flies elsewhere.

INT. LARGE DINING ROOM - DAY

A large round table sits in the middle of the dining-room.

ShaLann directs two male and female Iraqi Kurds to tape Thanksgiving drawings to the dining room walls.

ShaLann gives the Kurdish nationals a thumbs up when they're done. They smile and return ShaLann's thumbs up.

ShaLann and the Kurds place small bowls of snacks on a console in the room.

SERGEANT BUCKY enters the dining room and grabs a handful of nuts.

                    SHALANN
          Bucky I have a couple of hours
          before the turkey is done. Is it
          safe for me to take a short walk
          around the Compound to get some
          air?

                    SEARGEANT BUCKY
          Sure. We have a parameter set
          up and a partnership with the
          Kurds. You'll be fine.

EXT. COMPOUND GROUNDS - DAY

ShaLann can finally see the natural beauty of the country. ShaLann sees mountains, trees, a stream and a Mosque in the distance.

                    SHALANN (V.O.)
          It's a shame that a place so lovely
          is being destroyed by war.

ShaLann strolls along a body of water near the
Compound.

She walks less than ten minutes before she
comes across a group of armed men. A KURDISH
SOLDIER greets her.

                    KURDISH SOLDIER
          Hello.

                    SHALANN
          Assalamu alaykum.

          Translation: Peace be upon you.
          Are you the Kurdish rebels?

                    KURDISH SOLDIER
          Assalamu alaykum salam.
          Yes. We are them.

                    SHALANN
          Sad to hear of what Saddam has
          done to your people.

                    KURDISH SOLDIER
          Yes many of my family killed. Very
          sad.

                    SHALANN
          I pray that your life gets better.

                    KURDISH SOLDIER
          Thank you.

                    SHALANN
          Can I get a picture with you guys?

                    KURDISH SOLDIER
          Yes.

ShaLann stands front and center of the group
of soldiers while one of the soldiers takes a
few pictures.

                    SHALANN
          Thanks! You guys are famous in the
          United States.

                    KURDISH SOLDIER
          Famous?

                    SHALANN
          Yeah like movie star famous.

                    KURDISH SOLDIER
          Oh?

                    SHALANN
          Well I have to go back to the
          Compound.

The Kurdish soldier points in the direction of
the Compound.

ShaLann places her right hand over her heart
and slightly bows her head.

                    SHALANN (CONT'D)
          Peace be with you brothers.

The Kurdish Rebels put their hand over their
heart and nod to her.

                    KURDISH SOLDIER
          Peace be with you.

INT. COMPOUND - DAY

KITCHEN

ShaLann puts the final touches on the Thanksgiving dinner before one of the kitchen staff members carries it into the dining room.

DINING-ROOM

ShaLann directs the Kurdish nationals how to set up plates and utensils for formal dining.

Soon dignitaries from the State Department and a politician arrive for dinner.

We bow our heads and give grace.

The BRITISH COLONEL sharpens a large cutting knife.

A DIPLOMAT is looking puzzled at the beautifully dressed one-legged Turkey on the platter.

                    DIPLOMAT
          Excuse me Colonel why does the
          turkey have one leg?

                    BRITISH COLONEL
               (ponders answer)
          Landmine.

Everyone bursts out laughing.

                    SHALANN (V.O.)
          Oh that's frickin'
          hilarious. We're about to
          eat a bombed out warbird.
          May we be spared chipped
          teeth and a gut full of
          shrapnel.

COMPOUND FAMILY ROOM

An EGYPTIAN SOLDIER and FRENCH SOLDIER talk trash about the American football teams.

                    EGYPTIAN SOLDIER
          The Lions will get the win
          this time.

                    FRENCH SOLDIER
          Oh you are crazy!

                    SHALANN
          You guys are into American
          football?

                    FRENCH SOLDIER
          No. I'm into taking American
          money.

The U.S. soldiers laugh.

An AMERICAN SOLDIER walks around with a hat in
his hand.

                    AMERICAN SOLDIER
          Alright fellas put your money
          where your mouth is. Drop it in
          the hat. Hey Bucky write down
          the bets.

                    BUCKY
          Who you got Moore?

                    SHALANN
          I'm from Detroit so I'm going
          with the home team. What up doe?

                    FRENCH SOLDIER
          Ha-ha! I'll be happy to take
          your money too.

                    SHALANN (V.O.)
          We watch the game. A glimmer of
          hope fades fast when the Lions
          snatch defeat from the jaws
          of...well I lost my money.

The French soldier is smiling while he counts his money.

> FRENCH SOLDIER (CONT'D)
> What is it that you said? What
> up doe? My bank account.
> Hahhahahhaha!

The French soldier continues to laugh as he leaves the room.

ShaLann side eyes the French soldier on his way out the door.

> SHALANN (V.O.)
> Dammit! I come all the way
> to Iraq to get clowned by a
> French dude.

COMPOUND SHOWER ROOM - MORNING

ShaLann swings a dark wood door into what others call the shower room. Directly in front of her is a shower head and faucet handles.

To her right, a bucket, mop and cleaning supplies sit in a corner.

ShaLann walks in and closes the door behind her. She sits her shampoo and other toiletries on the floor.

The only closure on the door is a twisted hanger fashioned into a flimsy makeshift latch.

ShaLann decides to hum and sing to alert others that she is in the shower.

She washes and rinses her hair in the warm water.

ShaLann hears someone jiggle the handle on the door.

> SHALANN
>
> Occupado.

ShaLann doesn't hear footsteps walking away from the door so she assumes someone is still there. She unscrews the cap on a bottle of shampoo then pours a bit into her right hand.

The door slowly swings open into the shower room where ShaLann is standing there naked.

A tall good looking White BRITISH GUY pokes his head in.

> BRITISH GUY
> (calmly)
> Would you like some company?

> SHALANN
> (calmly)
> No thank you.

The British soldier slowly runs his eyes over ShaLann's naked body before he closes. The door.

ShaLann relaxes her body and breathes a sigh of relief.

> SHALANN (CONT'D)
> (whispers)
> Crap!

She uses the mop to seal the door. She braces the head of the mop between pipes to the left and the end of the handle against a pipe on the right.

> SHALANN (V.O.)
> It's a damn shame that on
> the safe side of the war
> zone I can't tell friend
> from foe.

COMPOUND GUEST BEDROOM

ShaLann sits on her bunk wearing jeans and a
sweat shirt. She pulls on her combat boots then
begins to lace them up.

BUCKY knocks on the open door.

> BUCKY
> Some of us are about to
> head into town to do a
> little Christmas shopping.
> You wanna go?

> SHALANN
> Sure.

A thirty-something-year-old white male CIVILIAN
GUARD dressed in Soldier of Fortune attire
appears in the doorway.

> SHALANN (V.O.)
> I don't recognize the guy, oh
> but damn sure recognize his
> spirit.

> CIVILIAN GUARD
> Of course she wants to
> go. All women love to
> shop.

The civilian guard looks down at ShaLann's
combat boots.

                    CIVILIAN GUARD
          Oh good. You're wearing
          sensible shoes.

                    SHALANN (V.O.)
          Sensible shoes! Did this
          sexist jerk just refer to my
          combat boots as sensible
          shoes? I just woke up, but
          I'm already tired of this
          sexist bullcrap.

INT/EXT. WHITE VAN - DAY

ShaLann, a small group of soldiers and a
civilian guard take a van to the local outdoor
market.

The roadways are mostly rough and unpaved.

ShaLann observes some women fully covered from
head to toe and others modestly dressed with
only their hair uncovered.

Every now and then the van passes a man with a
rifle slung over his shoulder.

The entire area looks poor and rundown.

                    SHALANN (V.O.)
          Man this place looks bad.
          It's as rundown as Detroit
          was after the riots of 1968.

EXT. OPEN AIR MARKET - DAY

ShaLann and the rest of the small group exit
the van in front of an open market.

                    CIVILIAN GUARD
          Welcome to the Red Zone.

SHALANN
The Red Zone? I don't want to
be a buzz kill, but Isn't it
illegal to have female troops
in this area?

CIVILIAN GUARD
Yeah, but we'll be in and out
real quick.

SHALANN (V.O.)
This place is giving me a
sinking feeling. My gut is
telling me that some hell can
jump off at any moment. It
doesn't help that I'm unarmed.

ShaLann purchases a gold teapot, some scarfs
and other nick-knacks. She haggles with the
vendor over a scarf.

A WOMAN IN BLACK, covered in a black Burqa from
head to toe approaches ShaLann on her right.

ShaLann can see the movement of something
pointy gradually protruding beneath the
woman's dress, near her abdomen.

WOMAN IN BLACK
Money!

SHALANN (V.O.)
Okay that sounded like a
demand; not a request.

ShaLann looks closer at the shape of the object
beneath the woman's garment.

Just in case it's a knife, ShaLann calmly wraps
the ends of a long scarf around each hand then
picks up the gold teapot with her right hand.

ShaLann can clearly see the tip of something too oddly shaped and pointy to be a fingernail.

Just as ShaLann begins to swing the teapot towards the knife things go haywire.

> CIVILIAN GUARD
> (screaming)
> KNIFE!

The guard grabs ShaLann by the back of her collar then slings her into the van.

ShaLann tumbles hard into the van; slamming the right side of her head against the frame around a window in the van.

ShaLann's gold teapot gets dented up in the melee.

> SHALANN (V.O.)
> In spite of the loud ringing
> in my ears and dizziness I
> can hear that this little
> shopping trip has gone
> completely off the rails.

The civilian guard is in a wild eyed rage; screaming and waving his M-16 around like a madman.

> CIVILIAN GUARD
> (yelling)
> Everybody get back!

Screams of terror erupt from women and children in the market.

> CIVILIAN GUARD(CONT'D)
> (yelling)
> I said get back or I'll
> frickin' kill every last
> one of you!

                    AMERICAN SOLDIER
                  (to American group)
              Get in the van now!

ShaLann tries to shake off the loud ringing
in her head. She feels herself fading so she
tries to keep herself from passing out.

The van races away from the scene at top speed.

INT. COMPOUND DINING ROOM- DAY

The team gathers near the dining-room table.

                    CIVILIAN GUARD
                  (yelling at ShaLann)
              Pay attention to your frickin'
              surroundings!

                    SHALANN
                  (sternly)
              I had her, but you jumped the
              gun!
                    CIVILIAN GUARD
                  (yelling)
              This is why women shouldn't
              be allowed on military
              missions!

                    SHALANN
              Right, because it would've
              been sooo much better for me
              to lose my crap and use the
              metal replacement for my
              manhood to terrify a bunch of
              women and children.

                    SHALANN (V.O.)
          Oops! As soon as the words left
          my mouth I knew I went too far.
          See penis insults land real
          different when a Black woman
          hurls them at a White man.

                    BRITISH COLONEL
               (yelling)
          Enough!

The civilian guard sneers at ShaLann.

ShaLann massages a pain in her right temple.

                    BRITISH COLONEL (CONT'D)
          Everybody pack up! We've
          picked up hot chatter so
          we're leaving the Compound.

                    SHALANN (V.O.)
          Good! I can't stand another
          moment with these un-
          friendlies in this so called
          safe zone.

INT/EXT. HELICOPTER - DAY

Two helicopters, with the call signs of Talons
Nest One and Talons Nest Two lift off from the
Compound.

ShaLann sits in Talons Nest One facing Chad
and the front of the craft.

ShaLann looks to her left and sees new faces:
An Air Force male and female, salt and pepper
haired TURKISH COLONEL and a TURKISH FIGHTER
PILOT.

ShaLann glances over at the Turkish Colonel.

ShaLann admires the countryside and the
mountains.

Soon it begins to snow outside. The snow falls
harder and harder. TALONS NEST ONE PILOT and
the TALONS NEST TWO PILOT engage.

                    TALONS NEST ONE PILOT (V.O.)
                (over headphones)
            Talons Nest One to Talons
            Nest Two, be advised. That
            snow forecast is starting to
            look a lot more like a
            blizzard.

                    TALONS NEST TWO PILOT (V.O.)
                (over headphones)
            Copy.

The snow is falling so hard that ShaLann can
no longer see the landscape or the mountains.

Over the headset ShaLann hears BEEP-BEEP BEEP-
BEEP.

ShaLann looks at Chad. He looks concerned.

                    SHALANN
            Chad you look worried.

                    CHAD
            We're being painted.

                    SHALANN
            Painted?

                    CHAD
            Saddam is painting our copter
            to launch a missile to destroy
            us. Our pilot is negotiating
            our survival.

> SHALANN (V.O.)
> What? Apparently our pilot is a
> silver tongued saint because
> our chopper flies threw the
> danger zone unscratched.

Darkness falls as the helicopters are flying.

The snow falls too.

> TALONS NEST ONE PILOT (V.O.)
> (over headphones)
> Talons Nest One to Talons Nest
> Two, zero visibility, terrain
> guidance authorized.

The copter drops a few feet and veers to the
left.

> SHALANN
> Now you look scared Chad.

> CHAD
> I am.

A crew member to the left of ShaLann and Chad
get up. The crew member hooks a cord to Chad's
belt then slides open the door to the copter.

Chad lays on his belly on the ground.

As the copter descends closer to the floor,
Chad hangs his upper body outside of the
helicopter.

ShaLann leans forward in her seat and grabs
Chad's right leg.

Chad calls out the topography of the terrain.

                    CHAD (V.O.)
                (over headphones)
          Railroad tracks sighted, go-head.

The copters continue to fly forward.

                    CHAD (V.O.)
                (over headphones)
          Telephone pole go up.

The copter ascends over the obstacle.

                    SHALANN (V.O.)
          Our pilot makes a decision
          to land in the blinding
          snow.

The copter ShaLann is riding in lands with a
jarring thud; jostling the crew members onboard.

The crew members of both helicopters get out
and survey their surroundings.

                    SHALANN (V.O.)
          Apparently we're lost around
          the borders of Syria, Iraq
          and Turkey.

Several of the crew members have their long guns
and side arms out.

ShaLann thinks she sees something move in the
distance.

                    SHALANN
          What's that ahead?

The crew members ready their weapons.

In the distance the crew can see figures
emerging between the darkness and the snow.

It's two men and four women from a nearby village.

ShaLann looks down and sees that the men have holes and large gaps in the sides of their shoes.

The women are holding something wrapped in dish towels.

                    TURKISH COLONEL
          Arabic: Marhaba
          Translation: Hello

One of the men wearing a sports jacket and sweater vest is the ARABIC SPOKESMAN for the group.

                    ARABIC SPOKESMAN
          Arabic: Raina tairtak
          alhalikoubter tenzel. Luqud
          jina lelemsade

          English translation: We saw
          your helicopter come down. We
          came to help.

One of the women steps forward to ShaLann and reveals steaming Arabic Pita bread.

ShaLann looks at the Turkish Colonel.

                    TURKISH COLONEL
          It's okay.

ShaLann looks the woman straight in her eyes then gives her a very serious look.

                    SHALANN (V.O.)
          Before I die, you're dead.

The woman returns a muted smile and a nod.

ShaLann breaks off a small piece of the bread
and puts it in her mouth. She smiles to the
woman.

                    SHALANN
          It's good.

The woman gives ShaLann a rotten teeth filled
smile.

The Turkish Colonel continues to talk to the
spokesman.

The Turkish Colonel turns to the helicopter
crew. He speaks in perfect English with a
soft European accent.

                 TURKISH COLONEL
               (to the crew)
          Unload the gear. We're
          going with them.

ShaLann pulls her green duffel bag from the
chopper and onto the snow covered ground.

The other male villager rushes over and helps
ShaLann with her duffel bag.

ShaLann looks up at the spokesman for the
villagers. He nods to ShaLann.

                 SHALANN (V.O.)
          I've met a few kingpins in
          my day, but I've never seen
          one wield power with holes
          in his shoes.

The crew and the villagers walk through ankle
deep snow towards a small village.

ShaLann walks next to the Turkish Colonel.

                    SHALANN
               (to Turkish Colonel)
          Sir isn't this the area that the
          terrorists were seen in?

                    TURKISH COLONEL
          These are the terrorists.

                    SHALANN
          Oh.

                    SHALANN (V.O.)
          Welcome to the crazy game of
          allies and villains. Watch
          your step. The good guys and
          bad guys exchange hats at
          will. It reminds me of home.

INT. THREE STORY HOUSE IN VILLAGE - NIGHT

Once inside the Turkish Colonel has a sit down
with the Leader of the Village.

ShaLann raises her camera and takes a picture
of the Leader of the House.

                    SHALANN (V.O.)
          Look at this guy. The Leader of
          the Village is sitting here
          smoking a cigarette like a
          villain in a Bond Movie.

The crew is led upstairs to a large carpeted
room with satin decorative covers and cushions
lining the walls.

LIVINGROOM

The crew sits down.

For the first time ShaLann can see most of the
crew members from the other helicopter.

ShaLann sits in the back of the room, facing
the door.

A row of four curtain-less windows line the
wall on ShaLann's left.

A woman enters the room and serves the crew tea.

A nine-year-old boy with a bad cough provides
the crew with plates and silverware then
leaves the room.

                    AMERICAN SOLDIER
          That boy needs some cough syrup.

                    SHALANN
          Or a doctor.

The nine-year-old boy returns. He uses two
hands to carry in a huge platter of brown
grains and turkey feet.

                    AMERICAN SOLDIER
          What is this?

                    TURKISH FIGHTER PILOT
          It's Bulger. It's like rice.

The Colonel joins the rest of the helicopter
crew members.

As soon as the Colonel sits down a crew member
enters the room and whispers to him.

                    SHALANN (V.O.)
          Unfortunately, one of the crew
          members can't locate his
          sidearm. I knew this was going
          a little too smooth.

                    TURKISH COLONEL
          Alright team let's bed down.

> We'll try to fly out of here at
> first light.

The crew unfurls the covers.

                    TURKISH FIGHTER PILOT
          You can sleep over here
          ShaLann.

                    SHALANN
          No thanks. I think I'll stay
          up and journal.

The Colonel bunks to ShaLann's left.

                    TURKISH COLONEL
               (whispering to ShaLann)
          I'll be awake too. Problems.

                    SHALANN
               (whispering to Colonel)
          Yeah I heard that a guy lost
          his firearm. You worried
          someone will find it and use
          it on us?

                    TURKISH COLONEL
          Yes, that and we're in a very
          bad area. I thought you
          should know this.

EXT. RIVER NEAR VILLAGE - NIGHT

BEGIN TURKISH COLONEL'S DAYDREAM

The Colonel envisions an aerial view of a
partially snow covered river.

                    TURKISH COLONEL (V.O.)
          We landed on the wrong side
          of the river inside of Syria.

He envisions a rough landing of a helicopter
on the edge of the river without hitting
trees.

                    TURKISH COLONEL
              There's no road out and we
              can't walk everyone across the
              shaky bridge the guards used.

END TURKISH COLONEL'S DAYDREAM

                                        BACK TO:

INT. LIVING ROOM - NIGHT

                    SHALANN
              I see.

                    TURKISH COLONEL
              Let's pray that we leave before
              the enemy knows we're here.

The Colonel removes a revolver from his jacket.
He opens the side and shows ShaLann that the
gun is fully loaded.

                    TURKISH COLONEL
              Here take my back up.

The Colonel snaps the bullet cartridge back
into place then tucks the weapon under
ShaLann's pillow.

                    TURKISH COLONEL
              I called the Turkish
              Jandarm to watch over us.

Two Turkish men carrying M-16s enter the room.

                    TURKISH COLONEL
              Here they are now.

ShaLann watches the Jandarm guards take a
position in the corner; on ShaLann's left side
of the room.

                    TURKISH COLONEL
          If the shooting starts, fire at
          the door then go out the window.
          We're on the second floor so
          bend your knees when you hit
          the ground.

                    SHALANN
          Yes sir.

ShaLann looks at the row of windows on her left.

                    SHALANNN (V.O.)
          Shoot and go out the window? How
          does that work? Do I go out the
          window shoulder first? Booty
          first? Kick the window out, sit
          on the sill and kind of scooch
          out while I'm shooting? Bend my
          knees when I hit the ground? And
          if I make it, where the Hell am I
          going?

The American Soldier is laying on the floor in
front of ShaLann.

                    AMERICAN SOLDIER
          I'm not worried about it. If it
          goes down, hopefully they'll
          kill me in my sleep. Ha-ha! I'm
          just kidding.

ShaLann blankly stares at the American Soldier.

The American Soldier turns his back to ShaLann
then goes to sleep.

ShaLann looks over at the Turkish Jandarm. The two guards are holding on to their gun barrels with their heads resting on their hands.

ShaLann glances out of the windows and watches the snow fall before returning to her journaling.

                              DISSOLVE TO:

EXT. SNOW COVERED GROUND NEAR HELICOPTER - DAY

The pilot from Talons Nest Two has the crews from both choppers stretched out in a straight line facing the helicopter.

They stand in shin deep snow awaiting further instructions.

                    TALONS NEST TWO PILOT
               Alright folks, we need to find
               this weapon. Gingerly slide
               your feet through the snow.
               Yell out if you feel an object.

                    AMERICAN SOLDIER
               Or a landmine.

The American soldier starts walking.

                    AMERICAN SOLDIER (CONT'D)
               Though I walk through the
               valley of the shadow of death
               I shall fear no evil...

ShaLann starts walking too.

                    SHALANN (V.O.)
               Good Lord this dude is really
               starting to suck. This mission
               sucks. And the Chief sucks
               donkey dicks. Oh well...

ShaLann begins to slide her feet.

                    SHALANN
          Thy rod and thy staff comfort me.

                         SOLDIER NEAR HELICOPTER
                    (yelling)
          I found it! It was at the foot
          of the stairs the whole time!

                         TALONS NEST TWO PILOT
          Alright everybody, load up!

INT/EXT. HELICOPTER - DAY

Both crews file into their respective
helicopters.

ShaLann is back in her seat facing Chad.

The pilots power up the helicopters. Gusts
of high winds combined with the force of air
from the rotor blades kick up a curtain of
blinding snow.

                         TALONS NEST ONE PILOT (V.O.)
                    (over headphones)
          Talons Nest One to Talons Nest Two.

                         TALONS NEST TWO PILOT (V.O.)
                    (over headphones)
          Comeback.

                         TALONS NEST ONE PILOT (V.O.)
                    (over headphones)
          We're gonna try the first puddle jump.

                         TALONS NEST TWO PILOT (V.O.)
                    (over headphones)
          Copy that.

Talons Nest One lifts off.

ShaLann can feel that the helicopter is shaking harder than before due to the high winds.

ShaLann grips the edge of her seat so tight that her knuckles turn white.

> SHALANN (V.O.)
> Helicopters weren't meant to fly this low or slow, but if the pilot flies forward too fast we could hit a bunch of trees. Too slow and we drop.

ShaLann can feel the helicopter shaking even harder.

ShaLann can feel the helicopter quickly descend.

The helicopter lands with a hard, jarring THUD!

The crew is abruptly jostled hard in their seats.

> TALONS NEST ONE PILOT (V.O.)
> (over headphones)
> Talons Nest One to Talons Nest Two, puddle jump successful.

The crew members on Talons Nest One relax and breathe a sigh of relief.

The passengers on Talons Nest One nod and smile at each other with unspoken gestures of gratuity for surviving a dangerous aerial maneuver.

Chad unbuckles his seatbelt.

                    CHAD
          Who wants breakfast?

                    SHALANN
          You guys had the good stuff
          and we ended up eating grains
          and turkey feet?

                    CHAD
          We didn't want to offend our hosts.

                    SHALANN
          I get that, but you could've
          slid me one of those packs to
          eat on the Q.T.

                    AMERICAN SOLDIER
          Hey Moore. Spaghetti or beef stew?

                    SHALANN
          Spaghetti.

EXT. WOODS NEAR HELICOPTER - DAY

ShaLann stands outside of the helicopter
stretching her arms and legs.

                    SHALANN
          I'm gonna head a little
          ways up this trail to
          freshen up. Any animals in
          these parts?

The Colonel shakes his head no.

ShaLann grabs a bottle of water and her shower
kit then walks a few yards up a walk path.

The trees managed to block most of the snow;
leaving many patches of the grounds untouched
by snow.

ShaLann scrunches up her nose when the stench of rotting death hits her nostrils.

> SHALANN (V.O.)
> This smells worse than the raw rotten chicken parts my instructors hung from trees during wartime mortuary affairs training.

She sees a one story red brick building ahead of her. It looks like an old roadside toilet hut at a small town rest stop.

The stench of death grows stronger with each step closer to the brick structure.

ShaLann steps off the path.

She walks a few feet to her left then stops near a big tree.

ShaLann rubs the injured area of her head with her right hand.

> SHALANN (V.O.
> Goose egg. Dammit!

ShaLann squats behind a tree to pee.

She constantly looks around for intruders or wild animals in the woods.

ShaLann pulls a baby wipe from her shower kit and cleans her undercarriage.

She tosses the wipe on a low mound of dirt.

She pulls up her trousers.

She walks back to the walk path.

ShaLann wets her toothbrush with bottled water then begins to brush her teeth.

Creek-Crick-Crack! Creek-Crick-Crack!

ShaLann hears sounds coming from the direction of the toilet hut. She carefully scans the area near the toilet hut, but doesn't see anything out of place.

From behind her.

Creek-Crick-Crack! Creek-Crick-Crack!

ShaLann turns back towards the helicopter, but she's startled when she stands face to face with the Turkish Fighter Pilot.

ShaLann removes her toothbrush from her mouth.

> SHALANN (CONT'D)
> Whoa!

ShaLann quickly palms the bristles of her toothbrush in her right fist. ShaLann doesn't wipe the toothpaste from her mouth. She silently stares at the Turkish Fighter Pilot.

> TURKISH FIGHTER PILOT
> My name is Armad. I like
> fiery beautiful women. No
> disrespect.

He swiftly steps forward, kisses ShaLann on her toothpaste covered mouth then quickly steps back.

> TURKISH FIGHTER PILOT
> Again no disrespect.

ShaLann looks stunned.

                    SHALANN (V.O.)
          What the? On one hand I want
          to shank this dude in both
          of his eyes with my
          toothbrush, but on the other
          hand that was kind of sweet.

The Turkish Pilot scrunches up his nose.

                    TURKISH FIGHTER PILOT
          You smell that?

He slowly walks towards the toilet hut.

ShaLann uses the baby wipe to remove the
toothpaste from her mouth.

                    SHALANN
          It's probably a dead animal.

The Turkish Fighter Pilot slowly walks towards
the brick toilet hut.

He covers his mouth and nose with his left
hand as he gets closer to the building.

He cranes his neck to see what's inside of an
open door to the toilet hut. He peeps in, then
quickly turns his head.

ShaLann walks towards him.

                    SHALANN(CONT'D)
          Is it a dead animal?

                    TURKISH FIGHTER PILOT
          Worse.

He raises his right hand to ShaLann indicating
for her to halt.

ShaLann cranes her neck to see what he's looking at, but the Pilot's arm blocks most of her view.

ShaLann catches a glimpse of what looks like the dirty naked heel of a foot laying inside the doorway of the brick hut.

> TURKISH FIGHTER PILOT
> Stay back. You don't need
> to see this.

He turns to walk towards ShaLann, but abruptly stops when something on his left catches his eye.

He quickly squats down.

ShaLann quickly squats down too. She silently scans the area for trouble.

The Pilot points to his left towards a crater in the ground near a tree.

ShaLann sees the crater in the ground and streaks of naked wood on a nearby tree.

The Pilot tightens up his grip on the weapon beneath his jacket. He slowly scans around him.

He looks closely at the walk path leading back to the helicopter. Nothing.

The Pilot slowly sweeps his head to the right then stops. He fixes his eyes on a naked low mound of dirt beneath a piece of white tissue laying on the ground.

> TURKISH FIGHTER PILOT
> (CONT'D)
> (whispering)
> Fresh landmines. There's one.
> See beneath that piece of white
> trash.

ShaLann sees it.

> SHALANN (V.O.)
> Oh crap, that's my butt
> wipe. It's a good thing I
> didn't bury it.

Sounds echo from the woods near the hut.
CRICK-CREEK-CRACK!

The Pilot reaches his right hand into the left
breast of his jacket. He grips the handle of
his holstered .45.

> TURKISH FIGHTER PILOT
> (whispering)
> Get behind me.

The Pilot turns to ShaLann.

> TURKISH FIGHTER PILOT
> Head back down the path.
> I'll follow you.

They start walking towards the helicopter. The
Pilot carefully scans the area along the way.

ShaLann sees a white van parked near the
helicopter.

> SHALANN (V.O.)
> Looks like the Calvary has
> arrived with our ride
> outta here. My gut tells
> me they're right on time.

                                        DISSOLVE TO:

EXT. TENT CITY INCIRLIK, TURKEY - DAY

ShaLann and one of the helicopter crew members
walk towards the Commander's Office in Tent
City.

A welcoming committee featuring The Chief, THE
COMMANDER, THE MAJOR (male) and SSgt Parker
stand in the yard in front of the Commander's
Office.

The Major is cradling a vase of fresh flowers
tucked in his left arm.

ShaLann stops in front of the welcoming party.

                    SHALANN
            Good afternoon Commander,
            Major, Chief, Parker.

The Major steps forward.

                    THE MAJOR
            Here are some flowers.

As soon as ShaLann takes the flowers and tucks
them in her right arm The Major embraces
ShaLann in a tight hug.

ShaLann looks stunned.

                    THE MAJOR (CONT'D)
            Oh thank goodness you made
            it! We were so worried!

The Major releases ShaLann from his hug.

                    THE MAJOR (CONT'D)
            Sorry I forgot myself.

                    THE COMMANDER
          At first I thought you were
          missing, but then I was informed
          that you were on dangerous
          missions in the Red Zone! How
          the heck did that happen?

The Chief squints her eyes at ShaLann then
subtly shakes her head no; indicating that
she wants ShaLann to be silent.

                    SHALANN (V.O.)
          I feel like punching this
          broad in the face.

ShaLann side eyes the Chief and shoots her a
dirty look.

                    SHALANN
                 (to the Commander)
          It was the Chief!

The Chief rolls her eyes then casts her gaze to
the ground.

ShaLann is angry.

                    SHALANN (CONT'D)
          She did it! I don't give a
          damn! I was almost stabbed,
          got a goose egg on-my-head
          and almost blowed up.

ShaLann starts walking away; shouting and
waving her hands as she walks.

                    SHALANN (CONT'D)
          Turkey feet and dead feet! I'm
          almost a marksman, but NO! I'm
          armed with shampoo, a teapot
          and a toothbrush! And somebody
          please get me some Motrin for
          this frickin' headache!

                    THE COMMANDER
          Chief, I need to see you in
          my office. Now!

                              DISSOLVE TO:

EXT. ENTRY GATE AT RHEIN MAIN AFB GERMANY - DAY

                    SHALANN (V.O.)
          The Chief was forced into
          retirement and I'm back in
          Deutschland.

INT. MILITARY HOSPITAL - DAY

ShaLann and four other PATIENTs sit in a row
of chairs in the Public Health Department.

To ShaLann's right is a closed door. Next to
it is a reception desk.

                    SHALANN (V.O.)
          If you thought my
          deployment nightmare was
          over guess again.

The closed office door opens.

                    SHALANN (V.O.)
          Turns out that kid with the
          cough who served us the
          turkey feet has TB. Now I
          have to go through six
          months of drug therapy.

A guy in a NAVY OFFICER appears in the open
doorway.

                    NAVY OFFICER
          Sergeant Paulski.

PATIENT
(to ShaLann)
Looks like the Squids are
running this drug treatment
program.

SHALANN
The Navy?

ShaLann looks to her right and sees the Navy
Officer.

ShaLann closes her eyes then tosses her head
back.

SHALANN (V.O.)
Frack my life!

INT. SHALANN'S KITCHEN - DAY

ShaLann is standing in front of her
refrigerator drinking water from a mug with
the words "THINK BIG" printed on it.

SHALANN (V.O.)
Shortly after the TB
treatment my health has
gotten pretty bad. If it's
not my stomach, odd rashes,
burning muscles or achy
bones, it's a headache that
makes my ears ring.

ShaLann's right arm and leg tremble
uncontrollably.

ShaLann falls to the floor unconscious.

The THINK BIG mug lays on the floor beside her
hand.

                    MED TECH'S VOICE (O.S.)
          She's going into Tachycardia!

                    SHALANN (V.O.)
          A stroke just destroyed one
          half of the communication
          sector in my brain. Due to
          declining health my military
          career is over.

A hand wearing a rubber glove stamps the words
MEDICAL RETIREMENT on a manila folder.

                              DISSOLVE TO:

EXT. TOPS OF GREEN TREES - DAY

Sunshine peeks through the rustling barren
branches of tall trees.

Howling winds swirl piles of Autumn leaves at
the snow covered feet of Oak Trees.

                    SHALANN (V.O.)
          Winter has fallen early.

INT. FUNERAL HOME - DAY

Prince Peter lays in a casket in a room filled
with chairs.

ShaLann dressed in a black dress and black
gloves walks up to her Father's casket.

                    SHALANN
          Well look at you Your
          Highness. All dressed up
          and ready to go.

ShaLann smooths down a wrinkle out of her
Father's blazer.

                    SHALANN (CONT'D)
          I thought I'd talk to you
          for a minute before your
          friends get here. I invited
          as many people from the
          Kingdom that I could find.

ShaLann plucks a piece of lint from her
father's sports coat then drops it to the
floor.

                    SHALANN (CON'D)
          As for me, I'm fine. My
          health seems to have
          stabilized. I'm living in
          Sin City now. Do you know
          that our Mayor used to be
          the Lawyer for Gangsters?
          And look at this.

ShaLann reaches into her purse and pulls out
a small blue passport.

                    SHALANN (CONT'D)
          I have a Diplomatic Passport.
          You should've seen me Father -
          dining and negotiating with
          Saudi Arabian Royalty. You
          would've been so proud.

ShaLann adjusts the gold, Cats Eye and Diamond
ring on her Father's right pinky finger. She
needs to show off his bling for his big day.

The doors open to the Receiving Room.

All manner of well-dressed old school players
and their ladies enter the room.

ShaLann gives the Eulogy in front of an
overflowing room of her Father's friends.

At the end of the service ShaLann shakes the
hands of the guests as they leave.

A middle aged Black WOMAN IN A LEATHER COAT
stops to talk to ShaLann.

                WOMAN IN A LEATHER COAT
      I hate to bring this up at
      this time, but what are you
      gone do with Pete's car?

                SHALANN
      I haven't decided yet.

                WOMAN IN A LEATHER COAT
      Pete would want me to have
      it. Here take my number. Call
      me when you get it from Alvin.

The woman hands ShaLann a small piece of paper.

ShaLann tucks the paper in the small black
handbag on her left arm.

The woman puts on a pair of large sunglasses
before walking out of the door.

ShaLann shakes hands with a couple more
people. A sixty-something-year-old Black MAN
IN BLACK MINK COAT stops to talk to ShaLann.

                MAN IN BLACK MINK COAT
      You probably don't remember
      me. I've worked with your
      father from the beginning.
      We need to have a sit down
      to discuss a pressing
      matter.

                    SHALANN
        Knowing my Father, he'd
        trust you to handle that
        on your own, right?

                    MAN IN BLACK MINK COAT
        Right. Thank you. Be blessed.

The man in the mink coat walks out the door.

                    SHALANN (V.O.)
        This is how it starts.
        There's no way in Hell I'm
        getting sucked into my
        Father's business!

The last man in line is a middle aged Black
guy named ALVIN. He's wearing an out of date
seer sucker suit that appears to be one size
too big for him. He stops to talk to ShaLann.

                    ALVIN
        I heard people talkin'
        about Prince Peter's car.

He flinches when he sees ShaLann reach into
her purse.

Alvin throws up his hands.

                    ALVIN (CONT'D)
            (scared)
        I don't want any trouble!
        He gave me the keys when
        his eyes got bad. I took
        him to the doctor.

ShaLann removes $100 in twenties from her purse
then puts the money in Alvin's left hand.

                    SHALANN
        Here's some gas money. Maybe get
        yourself a shrimp dinner.

Alvin gives ShaLann a wide smile.

                    ALVIN
        Oh thank you! Bless you!

                    SHALANN
        I'll let the woman know the
        car was willed to you.

                    ALVIN
        Thank you so much!

Alvin walks out of the door.

                    SHALANN (V.O.)
        Like I said I want no part of
        this business, but my Father
        hated pettiness and so do I.
        Now it's time for me to get
        back to my business.

END PRIMARY FLASHBACK

                              DISSOLVE TO:

INT. SHALANN'S HOUSE - DAY (PRESENT DAY)

BEDROOM

ShaLann sits at desk typing a line on her lap
top.

                    SHALANN (V.O.)
        Time to take a writing break.

ShaLann gets up from her desk.

She feels dizzy. She rubs her forehead when she swoons.

> SHALANN (V.O.)
> Whoa.

KITCHEN

ShaLann pours a bag of popcorn into a clear glass bowl.

ShaLann begins to walk up a flight of carpeted stairs.

When ShaLann reaches the middle of the staircase she feels light headed again, but this time she starts to black out.

ShaLann drops to her knees.

> SHALANN
> (breathless)
> Oh Father, help me.

The bowl of popcorn tumbles from her left hand as her body collapse's forward onto the stairs.

ShaLann hears her Father's voice in her head.

BEGIN CHILDHOOD FLASHBACK/VISION

EXT. SIDEWALK NEAR FATHER'S CAR - DAY (1968)

Five-year-old ShaLann trips on a crack in the sidewalk and falls hard on her left knee.

She cries and screams as blood pores from her wounded knee.

ShaLann sees her father's feet walk toward her. Her father reaches out his hand to ShaLann.

                    PRINCE PETER
          Get up Lann.

ShaLann is crying inconsolably. She shakes
her head.
                    LITTLE SHALANN
          No!
                    SHALANN'S GRANDMA (O.S.)
               (southern accent)
          Pick that chile up Pete!

                    PRINCE PETER
          Come on Lann. Remember, close
          your eyes real tight. Dig deep
          and get up Queen!

She envisions a finger moving in slow motion
as it hits keys on a laptop.

A fine mist puffs into the air and the loud
sound metal symbols crash each time a key is
struck.

G - The sound of symbols crash. Dust rises
from the "G" computer key.

E - The sound of symbols crash. Dust rises
from the "E" computer key.

T   - The sound of symbols crash. Dust rises
from the "T" computer key.

U   - The sound of symbols crash. Dust rises
from the "U" computer key.

P - The sound of symbols crash. SMOKE rises
from the "P" computer key.

END CHILDHOOD FLASHBACK/VISION

ShaLann thrusts her right arm into the air
then slaps the handrail with her right hand.

She pulls her upper body up until she's standing on her knees.

ShaLann raises her hands, palms towards her face before bending her head in silent prayer.

                              DISSOLVE TO:

INT. GROCERY STORE - DAY

A Pharmacy Technician hands ShaLann a white bag containing her prescriptions.

                    SHALANN (V.O.)
               It feels like my new meds
               are working.

ShaLann pushes a shopping cart down a grocery aisle.

When she reaches the end of the aisle she's surprised by an old friend.

                    SHALANN
               David!

David quickly hugs ShaLann.

                    DAVID
               Oh my goodness! How the
               heck have you been?

                    SHALANN
               Great! And you?

                    DAVID
               Awesome! Small world huh?

                    SHALANN
               For real!

A RED HEADED WOMAN and her young daughter walk up and stand on the left side of David.

                    RED HEADED WOMAN
              (to ShaLann)
     Hi.

                    SHALANN
     Hello.

                    DAVID
     This is my wife and daughter.

David's wife side eyes David.

                    SHALANN (V.O.)
     I would've side eyed
     David too if he
     introduced me without
     giving my name. Go on
     butt-head. This should be
     interesting.

                    DAVID
     ShaLann and I used to be
     stationed together.

                    SHALANN (V.O.)
     Oh okay. I'm not even his ex-
     girlfriend in this scenario.

                    SHALANN
              (to David's wife)
     Pleasure to meet you.

ShaLann looks at DAVID'S DAUGHTER.

                    SHALANN (CONT'D)
              (to the daughter)
     How old are you little one?

                    DAVID'S DAUGHTER
     Nine.

ShaLann purses her lips before looking at
David with disgust.

                    SHALANN
              (to David's wife)
          I have an appointment
          so I need to get out
          of here. It was a
          pleasure meeting you.

                    THE RED HEADED WOMAN
          Nice meeting you.

EXT. MILITARY GROCERY STORE PARKING LOT - DAY

As SherLann is putting a bag of groceries into
her trunk a roll of paper towels falls to the
ground. The paper towels roll down the
pavement of the parking lot.

David stops the roll of paper towels with his
right foot.

He bends down and picks up the package then
hands it to ShaLann.

                    DAVID
          Almost got away from you.

                    SHALANN
          Thank you.

David walks ShaLann to her car.

                    DAVID
          We should get together
          sometime. Keep it on the
          low like we used to do in
          Alaska.

                    SHALANN
               (annoyed)
          David, was that woman
          pregnant when you asked
          me to marry you?

                    DAVID
          I found out about that after
          I proposed to you.

                    SHALANN
          Oh my God!

ShaLann opens her car door.

                    DAVID
          So I take it that's a no?

                    SHALANN
          That's a Hell no and good bye!

INT/EXT. SHALANN'S CAR - DAY

                    SHALANN (V.O.)
          Looks like I dodged a
          bullet. Turns out he is
          just another greedy jerk.

She puts on a pair of big sunglasses then
backs out of the parking space.

INT/EXT. LAS VEGAS STRIP - DAY

ShaLann drives down the Las Vegas Strip.

Mariah Carey's Anytime You Need a Friend is
on the car radio.

                    SHALANN (V.O.)
          Although I'm still limping
          along with my health I
          finished my script. Heck,
          I actually finished a few
          of them and some books
          too. I guess I'm stronger
          when broken.

INT. AWARDS AND BOOK SIGNING EVENTS - NIGHT

BEGIN MONTAGE

- A poster of a screenplay titled LEAPERS
  appears on the screen. It has over fifteen
  movie laurels above a picture of a scary
  humanoid claw dragging a boot covered foot.

- A certificate with a woman with blood on a
  black bra and cleavage appears on the screen.
  The words "BEST IN FEST Boobs and Blood
  International Film Festival" appears beneath
  it.

- A certificate with a gold statuette appears
  on the screen. The words "BEST HORROR
  SCREENPLAY" appears beneath it.

- A purple book with a gold award seal on it
titled
  WICKED PRAYERS appears on the screen. The
  words "1st Prize in HORROR - READERS
  FAVORITES"

- A Picture of ShaLann wearing a black hat at
  a book signing appears then two seconds
  later disappears.

- A picture of Rance aka Randy Ran appears
  on the right side of the credits. "R.I.P.

Randy Ran" appears beneath the picture.
The picture disappears.

-   A picture of Ricky aka Maserati appears on
    the right side of the credits. "R.I.P.
    Maserati Rick" appears beneath the picture.
    The picture disappears.

-   A picture of Prince Peter in his Army uniform
    appears on the right side of the credits.
    "R.I.P. Prince Peter" appears beneath the
    picture. The picture disappears.

-   A picture of five-year-old ShaLann in a
    medium blue suit and white Go-Go boots
    appears then two seconds later disappears.

-   A picture of ShaLann wearing a parka standing
    in front of a helicopter appears then two
    seconds later disappears.

-   -A picture of a dented gold teapot with
    Arabic writing on it appears then two seconds
    later disappears.

-   -A picture of ShaLann wearing her Air Force
    blues appears then two seconds later
    disappears.

-   ShaLann thrusts a trophy into the air with
    her right hand. People in the audience
    give ShaLann a standing ovation.

                    THE END

SCREENPLAY ANALYSIS

1. What did you think of the dramatic and action pacing in the script?

2. Are the main characters notable and well written?

3. Are the sub-characters and scenes relevant?

4. Is the dialogue realistic?

5. What did you think of the overall implementation of the story in screenplay format?

WRITE A MOVIE SCENE STARRING YOU

You've learned basic script structure and what a story looks like in script format, now it's time to apply what you've learned. Write the first scene of a movie where two space aliens secretly observe you doing normal human things at home. The aliens will have an off screen (O.S.) speaking role, but their human subject will not.

Here's the set up: Two space aliens named **Beta** and **Karvac,** use an intergalactic viewing device to secretly observe humans in their homes. Beta has been monitoring people for three days. Although Beta is clueless about what the human is doing, names of human body parts or the names of the devices the human uses, Beta is considered a pro in explaining human behavior. Now Beta has been assigned to train Karvac in the ways of their human subject - **YOU**. Karvac have lots of questions for Beta about the things **YOU are doing** in your home. Beta will of course respond with wrong answers.

1. Write the scene in present tense.

2. Use a scene heading. If the camera has to observe you in a different room, use a mini scene heading.

3. Remember to capitalize the NAME of a character in the action element just before the character initially speaks in the script.

4. Also remember that this a movie scene so SHOW in action, DON'T TELL in dialogue. Example, you would state that Sally heats a pot of soup on the stove in the action element.

5. Remember the basics:

> Opening transition: FADE IN
> Action set up
> Scene Heading
> Action
> Character
> (Parenthetical if needed)
> Dialogue, (O.S.)

WRITE A SCENE STARRING YOU CONT.

FILM FESTIVALS

Red carpets, celebrities and parties - oh my! As you can tell from the laurels on the cover of this book my scripts won, became finalists or were accepted into many film festivals. I'm also a judge on a panel of a popular film festival so I kind of know my way around the circuit.

-Make sure to copyright your work and or register it with the Writers Guild of America (WGA) before entering a film festival.

-When it comes to entering film festivals, get feedback from at least two fests to see if there is a pattern of flaws that you need to address in your script. You also want to get a feel for how well your story is being received before exposing your work to top award qualifying film festivals.

-Attending live festivals gives you an opportunity to network with other writers, producers and directors. Bigger isn't always better. I snagged some great swag and made important connections at some smaller fests.

-Lastly, the film festival placement of my dramatic autobiographic feature script, Stronger When She's Broken film studio sponsored fests landed me meetings with two producers of some famous television shows and movies. Luckily I was ready to pitch my script.

PITCHING AND THE PITCH DECK

A pitch is a brief overview of what your screenplay is about. A pitch is usually presented verbally with or without visual or audio aids. A popular pitching aid is a pitch deck. It's a paper or virtual slide summary of story and business elements of your screenplay. Remember that your deck should include more visual elements and less wordy explanations. A pitch deck can be created using a variety of software programs. I prefer using Power Point, but you can use whatever program that works best for you. Every pitch deck is uniquely designed and inspired by the writer's creativity.

A pitch deck should include the following elements:

- A poster of your script
- Opening quote from your script with scene related image
- Logline, synopsis and style of genre
- Pictures of your desired cast
- Pictures that closely match a few scenes from your script
- Estimated budget
- Estimated production schedule
- Closing quote from your script with related image

* Some pitch decks include a collection of posters of films closely related to the screenplay they're pitching.

How long should your pitch deck be? I've seen decks as short as five pages and as long as twenty-seven pages. Understand this, film execs and film investors are busy people so brevity is your best friend.

-Keep It Simple and Visual

-Keep It Lean and Visual

-Keep It Relevant and Visual

The next section includes an example of my pitch deck for my Best of the Fest award winning horror script, LEAPERS.

LEAPERS PITCH DECK: COVER

Create a poster for the cover of your pitch deck. I always have a poster created for my scripts. I use it to display awards from film festivals.

PITCH DECK: OPENING QUOTE

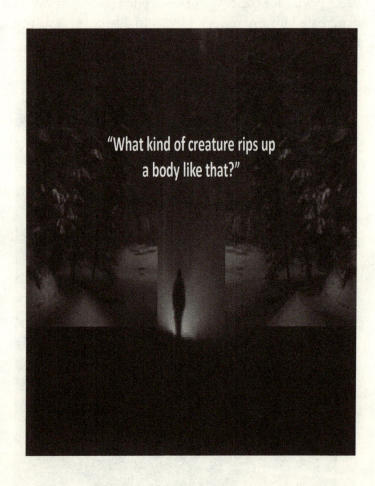

PITCH DECK LOGLINE AND SYNOPSIS

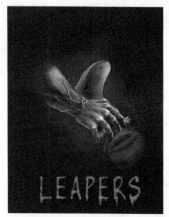

LOGLINE: An anniversary bash goes horribly wrong when supernatural, infectious Leapers crash the party.

SYNOPSIS: The Dean family throws an Anniversary party at their lodge in Alaska. A supernatural science experiment is unleashed near the lodge which births infectious creatures called Leapers.

The extra muscular creatures have powerful legs that allow them to pounce on their victims with frightening force. It doesn't take long before infected party guests become ferociously disagreeable. It's up to Jase, his girlfriend Rachel, his best friend Steve, his parents (Simone and Joseph Dean) and others to save the day.

Leapers harkens back to a time when action packed horror movies left the audience breathless with scary delight. Film festival professionals found the fight scenes "cheer worthy" and the scenes with Pogo and Fletcher "quite terrifying." The Pogo Leaper is a hulking man turned into a monster. The Pogo Leaper's demise opens the door for his resurrection. Film Festival professionals also found the overall story to be "haunting."

DREAM CAST AND CHARACTERS

 Jase Dean: Young Coast Guard Officer (W/M appx 30). He's a weapons lover and monster killer, but his guilt over a traumatic military mistake is unhelpful during a Leaper attack.

 Rachel: Jase's girlfriend (appx 30), Animal Biologist and Leaper fighting badass.

 Steve: Young Coast Guard Officer (B/M appx 30). He and Jase have been best friends since they were five years old. He has an artificial leg. Marksman.

 Simone Dean: Jase's Stepmom (B/F in Mid 50s). She's a tough, retired Professor of Animal Biology who kicks her some Leaper butt.

 Joseph Dean: Jase's Father (W/M in Mid 50s). He's an Army veteran going through a mid-life crisis. Saving his family from a monster attack is just what   this old warrior needed.

 Alicia: Steve's love interest (Asian/F appx 30). Being selfie addicted and gun shy during a Leaper attack is a very bad thing.

 Grand Poppa Joe: Jase's Grandfather (W/M 70) is a weed smoking, wise crackin' cuss who tends to skirt the law.

 Doctor Fletcher: Ambitious Research Scientist (Hispanic/M) whose recklessness unleash hell at the Dean's Anniversary party. Unfortunately, this player gets caught up in his game in the worst way.

 Pogo: Hulking good natured construction worker (Native American, over six feet) whose encounter with the Leapers is more than problematic.

 Frank: Construction Foreman (B/M) whose open secret is a pivotal moment in the fight against the Leapers.

214

PITCH DECK: MOVIE COMPARABLES

Add movie posters to show how your film compares to others. For this example, I'll use illustrations instead of proprietary images.

Lake Action Movie

Grrr Horror Movie

Wicked Prayers Horror Movie

PITCH DECK: THEMATIC MOOD

Use colorful images to show the thematic mood of your screenplay. Address inspiration for location, art, sound, lighting and unique visual effects.

PITCH DECK: PRODUCTION SCHEDULE

In this section you will use one to four pages to show investors how you intend to get it done. You will include an estimated production schedule, presumed costs of your music choices, location shoots, special effects/editing techniques, period for costumes and lighting like (insert pics from a movie (s) with a similar style. Here's an example. Although it's not a full list, it will point you in the right direction:

Pre-Production Costs

Production Crew: Long list

Cast: Actors, housing, rehearsals, contracts

Shooting Location: Facilities, permits

Equipment Rental: Vehicles to transport cast, costumes

FOOD: Meals and energy snacks

Production Schedule

Number of weeks for production

Principle shooting

Editing

Photography

Post Production

Music editing

Distribution

Marketing

PITCH DECK: CLOSING QUOTE

BONUS BOOK

WRITE IT!

ODD EXERCISES TO

HELP UNBLOCK

WRITER'S BLOCK

WRITER'S BLOCK?

After I sustained damage to half of the communication sector of my brain it took some effort to regain my writing abilities. Initially, everything that I wrote came out wrong. For example, in my mind I knew that what I wanted to say in writing were the words "the" or "very," but the words kept coming out garbled on paper as "hte" and "vrey." It was terribly frustrating. One day I remembered something from a human biology class that humans only use part of their brain. There was a vast amount of unused brain power to tap into. I tried closing my eyes and concentrating real hard to access those unused cells, but no luck.

I wondered what I could do to get my brain moving again. Bingo! The operative word was "moving." I remembered that the brain is a large complicated organ. I thought what's another complicated organ in the human body? The heart; which is also a muscle. The best way to get the heart moving is with exercise, but how could I exercise my brain? I tried reading math and science books, but that didn't work because my communications sector was damaged, therefore my comprehension was off too.

I decided to use more simplistic concepts of stimulation. The heart muscle usually responds to movement of the body or by experiencing emotions. Then I thought to myself, how can I move my body or provoke the right emotions to exercise my brain? The answer was to challenge my body to do things differently which in turn would challenge my brain to do things differently.

My initial goal was to be able to simply write basic sentences, but what I ended up with was a whole lot more.

At the end of these exercises you may find yourself further along with your story than before you began this course. The following are a few of the odd exercises I used to unblock my extreme case of writer's block.

UNBLOCK IT!

Since this program involves physical and emotional movements, please check with the necessary professionals before trying any of the exercises. Many may experience anxiety and or tiredness. Again, seek advice from a medical professional before proceeding. Some may become very tired so it's best that you not operate any heavy machinery until you've rested.

****

Supplies That You'll Need

*Most of these items can be acquired at a dollar store.

- Your everyday toothbrush
- A clean eating utensil
- Food that doesn't require being cut with a knife before eating it, but requires an eating utensil (yogurt, cereal, soup, etc)
- A pair of socks rolled into a ball
- Flat indoor area, free of debris to safely walk several feet in a straight path. (If in a wheelchair, the same rules apply)
- A place to sit and write as needed
- A stopwatch (most phones have one) or timer
- A location to take a nap because you'll likely get tired
- A large notebook with paper large enough to allow you to write paragraphs
- Ink pen
- A device that you can use to record your voice or image for signing for at least 60 minutes. Most phones have a recording feature.

GET TO KNOW YOUR CHARACTERS

Perform this exercise before dinner. Keep your answers brief. Brevity rules the day in screenwriting.

Keep it short.

Keep it simple.

Keep it relevant.

You will only identify three characters. Complete this exercise even if one of your characters is an object such as a haunted house or a soccer ball.

CHARACTER #1

NAME OF CHARACTER: _____

POSITIVE CHARACTER TRAITS: _____

_____

_____

NEGATIVE TRAITS: _____

_____

_____

CHARACTER'S FRIENDS: _____

_____

_____

CHARACTER'S ENEMIES: _____

_____

_____

PROS AND CONS ABOUT WHERE THIS CHARACTER LIVES? _____

_____

_____

CHARACTER #2

NAME OF CHARACTER:
_____

POSITIVE CHARACTER TRAITS: _____

_____

_____

NEGATIVE TRAITS: _____

_____

_____

CHARACTER'S FRIENDS: _____

_____

_____

CHARACTER'S ENEMIES: _____

_____

_____

PROS AND CONS ABOUT WHERE THIS CHARACTER LIVES?

_____

_____

CHARACTER #3

NAME OF CHARACTER:
_____

POSITIVE CHARACTER TRAITS:
_____

_____

_____

NEGATIVE TRAITS:
_____

_____

_____

CHARACTER'S FRIENDS:
_____

_____

_____

CHARACTER'S ENEMIES:
_____

_____

_____

PROS AND CONS ABOUT WHERE THIS CHARACTER LIVES?
_____

_____

_____

WHERE DO I BEGIN?

I recently received a message from a writer who has writer's block because he couldn't come up with a title for his script. He told me that he couldn't start writing his story because two of his characters need to say the title on first two pages. He said that there is no way that he can move forward without a title. My advice, use a place holder title. You can always change it later. Don't let less than ten words prevent you from writing thousands of words.

Another way to move beyond the "How do I begin" roadblock is to start with a fairytale beginning and flow from there. You can always clean up the beginning later, the key is to start and continue writing. Here are some examples of a fairytale beginning:

Once upon a sunny day my character…

Once upon a dreary night my character…

In the beginning, my character Jo Doe…

Jane Doe is having the best day of her life, but things turn when…

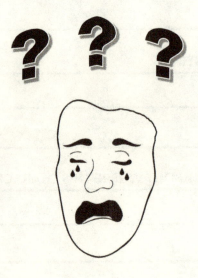

WRITE BACK TO FRONT

*For this exercise you will need your recorder.

When I was in the Air Force I had to attend four months of specialized training to learn how think and speak quickly on my feet. One of the exercises that I repeatedly completed was to create a story based on a single word that was assigned to me. I had five minutes to come up with a five-minute story that was composed of a beginning, middle and end. Almost everyone in my group struggled with coming up with a beginning, but almost everyone knew what the ending of their story would be.

I always found that whenever I try to craft the beginning of a story, my mind drifts to everything about the story except the first step. However, the last few steps of the story or the general goal is usually much clearer. In essence, knowing your destination is much easier to figure out than how you're going to get there. The destination could also be a state of mind like "They lived happily ever after" or achieved a position like the first one-armed Sheriff of Hambone Gulch. Your story has a destination too.

*****

Take out your recorder. Using a recorder will help you capture a greater degree of thought than writing down your answers.

Your word is ENDING. Use your recorder to answer the following questions.

1. Tell me about the ending of your story.

2. Tell me about the surroundings your characters are in (outside/indoors).

3. Tell me about the emotional outcome you hope to achieve.

NOTES ABOUT YOUR ENDING

As you recorded the responses to the ending of your story did you think of something new about your ending or something new about your story? Write down your discovery.

_____

_____

_____

_____

_____

_____

_____

_____

_____

_____

_____

_____

Focus and Relaxation

After I experienced an injury to the communication sector of my brain, I was verbally out of sorts. I couldn't mentally focus to spell words or stay on track with word tasks. Eventually I was able to spell again, but I improved my written communication skills. I can't guarantee that this will give you all of what I've gained, but it should help you improve your focus and tap into your creativity. No caffeine and or stimulants are allowed. You need to tap into your natural power.

The first step is to warm up the brain by doing things in opposite ways. You must begin the night before the writing exercises. The following exercises may make you feel a little weird, so it's best to try this on a night before a day off from major activities like work, childcare or operating heavy machinery.

Do the following before you begin the relaxation exercises:

A. Use your/nondominant hand to thoroughly brush your teeth.
B. Give a final check of your electronic messages.
C. Write down the names of your characters.
D. Place the list of your characters and a pen next to your bed.

*Do NOT check electronic devices UNTIL YOU have had some sleep.

*DO NOT CHEAT OR YOU WILL NOT ACHIEVE YOUR GOAL.

1. **LIGHTLY STRETCH BEFORE GOING TO BED.**
   Do not do these exercises if they are discouraged by
   your doctor or if you have been experiencing pain in
   the muscle groups.

   A. Steady yourself by placing your left hand on a table
   or back of a chair. Bend your right leg back and up.
   Use your right hand to help stretch your heel toward
   your buttock. Hold for 10 seconds. Now use your right
   hand to steady yourself. Use the previous steps to
   stretch your left leg. Hold for 10 seconds. Repeat the
   aforementioned steps.

   B. While standing, stretch your right arm and open hand
   up towards the ceiling. Hold for 10 seconds.

   Now switch and stretch your left arm and hand
   towards the ceiling. Hold for 10 seconds. Repeat the
   aforementioned steps.

2. Character Focused Deep Breathing:

- Sit on your bed cross legged
- Rest the back of your left hand on top of your left thigh near your knee and the back of your right hand on top of right thigh, near your right knee
- Think of the names of your main characters
- Close your eyes
- Inhale through your nose and hold your breath 5 seconds
- Exhale through your mouth
  Repeat this br7eathing exercise five times.

3. Bedtime:

The goal of this exercise is to naturally stimulate your brain to focus on the characters in your story without subconscious interference from someone else's screenplay.

If you sleep with the television on, <u>turn to a station that has music only.</u>

If you are having difficulty sleeping, close your eyes and envision your characters interacting as if they are in a movie. See your characters interacting indoors and outdoors.

If you dream of something new about your characters, write down as much as you can remember as soon as you wake up.

*Do NOT check electronic devices or watch TV UNTIL YOU GET SOME SLEEP. GOOD NIGHT!

Mental Workout

Before you begin the next set of exercises, please prepare you breakfast. After you've prepared your meal.

1. Use your nondominant hand to eat your food.

2. You have a total of one hour to eat, check your email, phon and or social media messages.

3. After your hour is up, it's time to brush your teeth. Floss Place tooth paste on your toothbrush.

Close your eyes and use your nondominant hand to thoroughl brush your teeth, mouth and tongue.

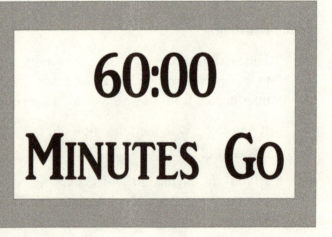

Mental Workout Continued: Sock Ball

For this exercise you will need a pair of socks or footies rolled up into a ball. You will need an area about 10 feet long that is clear of debris or breakable items.

*****

1. Pick up the ball of socks and stand in the 7-feet-long walking space.
2. **Toss and catch the sock-ball between your hands** for 30 seconds.
3. Toss the sock-ball between each hand as you walk forward 5 steps.
4. **Walk in the opposite direction** and repeat step 3.
5. Repeat steps 3 & 4 <u>five times</u>.

*****

1. <u>**Walk Backwards**</u> 5 steps as you toss sock-ball, counting to 5
2. Walk in the opposite direction as you repeat step 1.
3. Repeat steps 1 and 2 five times.
4. **Spread your hands further apart** by about two-three inches.
5. Repeat steps 1 and 2 <u>five times</u>.

*****

1. <u>**Close your eyes**</u>
2. While tossing the sock-ball walk seven steps backwards while counting aloud to <u>**7**</u>.
3. Repeat steps 1 and 2 <u>seven times</u>.
4. Next **spread your hands further apart** by about two-three inches.
5. Repeat steps 1 and 2 <u>seven times</u>.

*****

1. **Stop and put down the sock-ball.**
2. **Close your eyes and take a deep breath,** hold for 5 seconds and exhale. Repeat breathing exercise two more times.

233

FOCUS ON YOUR STORY

How will your main characters reach their goal?

Use your recorder to give an expanded summary of how your main characters will achieve their final goal. When you're finished recording, save your work and make any additional notes below.

_____

_____

_____

_____

_____

_____

_____

_____

_____

NOTES

SCENE NOTES

SCENE NOTES

_____

_____

_____

_____

_____

_____

_____

_____

_____

_____

_____

_____

_____

SCENE NOTES

SCENE NOTES

SCENE NOTES

CHARACTER NOTES

_____

_____

_____

_____

_____

_____

_____

_____

_____

_____

_____

_____

_____

CHARACTER NOTES

_____

_____

_____

_____

_____

_____

_____

_____

_____

_____

_____

_____

_____

CHARACTER NOTES

CHARACTER NOTES

CHARACTER NOTES

STORY NOTES

STORY NOTES

STORY NOTES

STORY NOTES

STORY NOTES

ANSWERS

1. Tina trips and breaks her leg. You are directing an actor to perform an action in present tense. Remember the script must be written in present tense unless a character is verbally recalling something.

2.   BRAD
  Johnny is running late.

3. Scene heading

4. By using a parenthetical to indicate behavior simultaneously occurring with a character's dialogue.

5.   JULZ
          (yawning)
  Oh man I'm exhausted.

6. Action

7. INT/EXT. CAB OF SEMI TRUCK - NIGHT

ANSWERS CONTINUED

8.

                    JULZ
        Mom sent over sausage and cheese
        trays for the opening our new
        recovery wing.

                    JADE
            Awesome! I'm starving.

    Jade rushes over to the refreshment table.

                    DAISY
            Me too.

    Daisy grabs a plate.

                    JAXX
            Now we can fully use our Med-
            School training in the tattoo
            shop.

    Joe pours a jar of cheese sauce into a plastic serving bow
    and then sticks a plastic spoon in the dip.

                    JULZ
                (annoyed - shouts)
            JOE!

                    JOE
            What? Nobody wants to mess around
            with mom's fancy, smancy iron
            sauce pots.

GLOSSARY

I Hope You Enjoyed the Learning Experience. Here's More About the Author

S.D. Moore is a multiple award winning author turned multiple award winning screenwriter. Moore's screenwriting awards include all of the awards on the front cover and more:

LEAPERS: Awards include Nominated for Best Fantasy in Hollywood Dreams/Action on Film Festivals 2021, Best of the Fest and Best Feature Script - Boobs and Blood 2020, Best Horror Screenplay – LAFA 2020, Best Original Story – Vegas Movie Awards 2020. FINALIST for Best Feature Screenplay in the following: Independent Horror Movie Awards 2021, California Women's Film Festival 2020, Zed Fest Film Festival & Screenplay Competition 2020, Feel the Reel International Film Festival 2020, 13 Horror.com Film and Screenplay Contest 2020 and more.

STRONGER WHEN SHE'S BROKEN: Awards include Cash, Winner on Best Written Work – Las Vegas Black Film Festival 2021, Winner of Best Feature Inspired by a True Story – Silver State Film Festival 2020 and Winner for Best Feature Screenplay – WIKI 2020. FINALIST and nominations from Hollywood Int Diversity Film Festival 2021, LA International Underground 2020, Feel the Reel 2020, Top Indie Awards 2021, Hip Hop Film Festival 2021 and more.

PERFECTLY NORMAL IN FLAGSTAFF: Las Vegas BFF – Best Adapted Work 2019, Best in Comedy – LV Screenplay Contest 2019, Silver Screen Award - Nevada Int Film Festival 2018.

WICKED PRAYERS NOVEL: First prize in BEST FICTION HORROR in the Reader's Favorites International Book Competition. The novel also earned an excellent review from KIRKUS Reviews.

S.D. Moore is also a former military, college and university instructor. Moore holds double Masters in Management and Human Resources Development and is a dissertation away from a Doctorate of Education. S.D. Moore is also the patented inventor of the Portable Hot Sink System.

www.ingramcontent.com/pod-product-compliance
Lightning Source LLC
LaVergne TN
LVHW092348030125
800401LV00001B/204